The Glamping Investor: A BiggerPockets Guide

The Glamping Investor

A BiggerPockets Guide
with Garrett Brown

BiggerPockets
PUBLISHING
Denver, Colorado

This publication is protected under the U.S. Copyright Act of 1976 and all other applicable international, federal, state, and local laws, and all rights are reserved, including resale rights: You are not allowed to reproduce, transmit, or sell this book in part or in full without the written permission of the publisher.

Limit of Liability: Although the author and publisher have made reasonable efforts to ensure that the contents of this book were correct at press time, the author and publisher do not make, and hereby disclaim, any representations and warranties regarding the content of the book, whether express or implied, including implied warranties of merchantability or fitness for a particular purpose. You use the contents in this book at your own risk. Author and publisher hereby disclaim any liability to any other party for any loss, damage, or cost arising from or related to the accuracy or completeness of the contents of the book, including any errors or omissions in this book, regardless of the cause. Neither the author nor the publisher shall be held liable or responsible to any person or entity with respect to any loss or incidental, indirect, or consequential damages caused, or alleged to have been caused, directly or indirectly, by the contents contained herein. The contents of this book are informational in nature and are not legal or tax advice, and the authors and publishers are not engaged in the provision of legal, tax or any other advice. You should seek your own advice from professional advisors, including lawyers and accountants, regarding the legal, tax, and financial implications of any real estate transaction you contemplate.

The Glamping Investor: A BiggerPockets Guide
Garrett Brown

Published by BiggerPockets Publishing LLC, Denver, CO
Copyright © 2025 by Garrett Brown
All rights reserved.

Publisher's Cataloging-in-Publication Data
Names: Brown, Garrett, 1990-, author.
Title: The glamping investor : a BiggerPockets guide / with Garrett Brown.
Description: Includes bibliographical references. | Denver, CO: BiggerPockets Publishing, LLC, 2025.
Identifiers: LCCN:2025935287 | ISBN: 9781960178923 (paperback) | 9781960178930(ebook)
Subjects: LCSH Camp sites, facilities, etc.--Management. | Hospitality industry--Management.| Real estate investment. | Real estate business. | Real estate development. | BISAC BUSINESS and ECONOMICS / Personal Finance / Investing | BUSINESS and ECONOMICS / Real Estate / General | BUSINESS and ECONOMICS / Industries / Hospitality, Travel and Tourism
Classification: LCC GV191.72 .B53 2025 | DDC 647.947309--dc23
Published in the United States of America
10 9 8 7 6 5 4 3 2 1

Dedication

To Cameron, Kayla, Mom, and Dad.
Your love, belief, and encouragement gave me the
strength to leap into something completely new.
None of this would exist without you.

BiggerPockets Guide Mission Statement

Revolutionize your investing journey with BiggerPockets Guides: a series of laser-focused, in-depth strategy blueprints designed to help you master crucial real estate topics. These books tackle advanced investing subjects head-on, providing you with trustworthy insights that will supercharge your real estate journey.

Say goodbye to expensive guru courses and flashy masterminds. BiggerPockets Guides are your *affordable* ticket to real estate success. We've distilled the valuable knowledge of real experts into accessible guides that connect you with even more free tools and resources on the BiggerPockets website.

Whether you're a seasoned pro or just starting out, our guides will be your secret weapon in helping you navigate the lucrative world of real estate investing with confidence. Get ready to transform your financial future—one guide at a time!

Prepare to Discover ...

... the exciting and rapidly growing glamping industry. This practical guide walks you through every aspect of the glamping industry, from market analysis and property acquisition to daily operations and future trends.

You'll learn how to:

- Build long-term wealth through strategic land and short-term rental development
- Identify and acquire prime glamping locations
- Select and implement profitable accommodation types and amenities
- Create memorable guest experiences through customer service and professionalism
- Anticipate problems with preventive maintenance
- Successfully market your glamping business
- The benefits and paths to scaling your glamping business

Table of Contents

Foreword. 10

Part 1: Foundations of Glamping 12

    Chapter 1: Understanding the Glamping Market. 13

    Chapter 2: Planning Your Glamping Business. 22

    Chapter 3: Finding a Glamping Property. 38

    Chapter 4: Funding Your Glamping Site. 48

Part 2: Setting Up Your Glamping Site. 65

    Chapter 5: Site Development 66

    Chapter 6: Accommodation Options. 77

    Chapter 7: Amenities and Facilities 89

Part 3: Operations and Management. 96

    Chapter 8: Daily Operations 97

    Chapter 9: Guest Experience Management 104

    Chapter 10: Property Maintenance for Glamping Sites 109

Part 4: Marketing and Sales 115

Chapter 11: Marketing Strategy. 116

Chapter 12: Distribution and Sales. 128

Chapter 13: Customer Relationship Management 139

Part 5: Financial Management 148

Chapter 14: Financial Planning 149

Chapter 15: Performance Metrics 160

Part 6: Growth and Innovation 169

Chapter 16: Scaling Your Business 170

Chapter 17: Future Trends in Glamping. .178

Chapter 18: The Glamping Journey Ahead. 185

Acknowledgments 187

About the Author. 188

Reference List. 189

Foreword

Glamping is more than just a trendy buzzword; it's a movement that blends the magic of camping with luxury comforts. Whether you call it glamorous camping, glorious camping, luxury camping, or something else entirely, one thing is clear and will be for years to come: People crave experiences that take them out of their daily grind and immerse them in something they can't experience every day.

My journey into glamping probably started a lot like yours—scrolling through social media, seeing some wild structure in the woods with an even wilder cash flow number attached. I remember thinking, *Wait . . . a tent can make me creative and rich? I'm in.*

What started as curiosity has turned into the most rewarding chapter of my life. Over the past four years, I've grown from one experiment to two fully operating sites—with two more on the way—all thanks to the returns we've earned and the brand we've built.

But don't let the dreamy views fool you—this business comes with its fair share of chaos. I've dealt with everything from goat sacrifices (don't ask) to floods and surprise alligator cameos. Still, I wouldn't trade this mix of real estate, hospitality, and storytelling for anything.

As urban areas face oversaturation in the short-term rental market, investors turn to rural and unique destinations for opportunities. This shift has opened the door to glamping—a buzzing industry that combines the charm of the great outdoors with creature comforts like memory foam beds, hot showers, actual bathrooms (not buckets or whatever tree you can find), fast Wi-Fi, and even air conditioning. While Europe has been leading the charge for years, the U.S. is finally catching up, and the potential here is limitless.

If you understand that glamping is a business model won on two fronts, real estate and the hospitality industry, you will create something rewarding. If you don't prepare on both sides, you will fail before you start. You have to pick the correct market, specific properties, proper guest avatar, hotel operations, and campground maintenance and navigate regulations that are not typical. This sounds like a lot to comprehend, but leaning on people who have navigated the process helped me understand each nuance of your new venture (*adventure* works too).

When I started my first glamping site, in 2021, I was equal parts excited and terrified. Mistakes? I've made them. Wins? Plenty of those too. This guide is your shortcut—the resource I wish I had had when I began—to help you navigate the glamping business with confidence, creativity, and a sense of adventure.

Part 1

Foundations of Glamping

Chapter 1

Understanding the Glamping Market

I remember the first time I saw a YouTube video about glamping sites and the "outrageous" returns you can get from just plopping some tents in the woods. I went down a rabbit hole of how this could be, as I was currently a short-term rental investor in Houston, struggling to break even. I have been in the Houston real estate market for over eight years, as a real estate agent and halfway investor. When I say "halfway investor," I mean I would try a few different strategies about halfway then lose interest. Fix-and-flip? Yep, one successful one and three fails. BRRRR? Yep, but I only pulled off one that was successful. I realized these were not sustainable for my own goals, and I decided to give short-term rentals (STRs) a shot.

My most successful deal actually came from my least favorite activity, cold-calling. I called "For sale by owner"s from Zillow almost daily when I focused on the sales side of being a real estate agent. I hated every minute of it, but I knew that listings weren't going to find me. I found an owner who had his three condos for sale and for lease and decided to try my luck. Joseph (the owner) ended up letting me list the properties for lease, and I found a tenant within a few days for all three.

This small task was not considered major by any means for me, but it put me on the path for my first STR deal. A year passed, and Joseph called me to sell his three condos. I had just acquired the STR itch and decided to ask him to sell me the condos instead. We worked out a great deal for both sides, and I immediately furnished the units for my first try at Airbnb.

The year 2018 was great, and we made around $100,000 in gross revenue for all three condos. But 2019 was not so great, as corporate money came into downtown Houston after hearing about the grab bag that was Airbnb at the moment.

It was then a race to the bottom in terms of pricing, and I couldn't compete with massive operations such as Sonder. I knew I needed to pivot, and I also wanted something more fulfilling. I am a creative person by nature, and seeing the same type of listings over and over on

Airbnb was beginning to kill my passion. When I started that glamping YouTube rabbit hole, I knew I had found a way to finally scratch that creative itch as well as a financial one. Luckily, I was correct, and we have been able to expand to eight units under management on two sites, earn a gross revenue of almost $800,000 a year, almost triple our real estate values from $550,000 to $1,300,000, and actively plan for our next expansion project. This guide will cover how exactly I did this with minimal financial backing and have become one of the most sought-after glamping destinations in Texas.

What Is Glamping?

Mention "glamping" to someone who's never heard of it, and you'll likely get a puzzled look. But say it to the right audience, and their eyes light up. *Glamping* is luxurious camping—a fusion of outdoor adventure and hotel-level comfort. What started with the humble beginnings of having a refrigerator inside a tent has now evolved into a competition for how far operators can take their vision.

Traditional campgrounds have been around forever, offering low-cost ways to use land with minimal infrastructure. But glamping has flipped that model on its head, turning camping into an upscale experience that appeals to a broader audience. Guests want the joy of nature without sacrificing comfort, and they're willing to pay a premium for it.

The global glamping market has experienced significant growth in recent years and is poised for continued expansion. In 2024, the market was valued at approximately $3.45 billion and is projected to reach $6.18 billion by 2030, reflecting a compound annual growth rate (CAGR) of 10.3 percent from 2025 to 2030. Regionally, Europe dominated the market in 2024, accounting for over 35 percent of the global share. North America also held a significant portion, with a 25 percent share in the same year.[1]

---

[1] "Glamping Market Size, Share & Trends Analysis Report by Accommodation (Cabins & Pods, Tents, Yurts, Treehouses), By Age Group (18 - 32, 33 - 50, 51 - 65, Above 65 Years), By Booking Mode, By Region, And Segment Forecasts, 2025 – 2030," Grand View Research, accessed 25 April 2025, https://www.grandviewresearch.com/industry-analysis/glamping-market#.

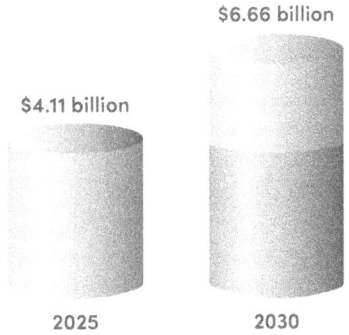

Glamping Market
Market forecast to grow at a CAGR of 10%

$6.66 billion — 2030
$4.11 billion — 2025

Source: https://www.researchandmarkets.com/reports/5716440

Who's Your Market?

Understanding your market and target guest avatar is essential. Think about your friends, your family, your local demographic, your regional demographic, and anyone who could be in your radius soon. Who is most likely to stay at your glamping site? Every location can be built for a different guest avatar, but you need to pinpoint your goals for that vision early on. While glamping appeals to many, the core demographic typically meets criteria.

- Age range: 28 to 40 years old, slightly skewed toward millennials
- Gender: Predominantly female. Women often book trips for families or couples.
- Key traits: Social media–savvy travelers who value unique experiences and sustainability

This trend is expected to grow even further as the generation behind millennials, Generation Z (born between 1997 and 2012), becomes a larger part of the travel market. This is way bigger than TikTok and Twitch. Gen Z travelers have distinct preferences that set them apart.

- **Experience over material goods:** Unlike previous generations, Gen Z prioritizes travel that offers memorable and Instagram-worthy experiences over traditional luxury accommodations.
- **Off-the-beaten-path destinations:** A survey by Condor Ferries found that 70 percent of Gen Z travelers actively seek unique travel experiences that their family and friends have not heard of.[2] This aligns perfectly with the glamping industry's focus on remote, immersive, and distinctive stays.
- **Eco-conscious choices:** Sustainability is a key driver for Gen Z. They prefer accommodations that prioritize eco-friendly practices such as solar energy, minimal waste, and locally sourced materials. Investing in sustainable features can increase a glamping site's appeal to this growing demographic.
- **Digital connectivity and booking preferences:** Gen Z expects seamless online booking experiences and often relies on peer reviews and social media to make travel decisions. Having a strong digital presence, engaging content, and positive guest reviews are critical to attracting this audience.

As this younger generation matures into the primary travel demographic, glamping businesses that cater to experiential, sustainable, and tech-forward travel preferences will have a competitive edge in the market.

Why Glamping Works

When I started my glamping company, Cameron Ranch Glamping, I had a strong passion for developing it with a purpose. I had heard about the profits that could potentially come in, but I also truly cared about the guest experience. I wanted to build a place where people could escape their urban jungles and come disconnect to reconnect with nature in a "luxury" setting.

Guests come for the novelty but stay for the experience. Glamping units are easy to market based on the design and elements already

---

[2] "Gen Z Travel Statistics, 2025," Condor Ferries, accessed 25 April 2025, https://www.condorferries.co.uk/gen-z-travel-statistics.

popular on social media and search engines. Guests will easily share your property as a form of "social currency" online with others and give you organic marketing that costs you nothing. A typical short-term rental (just a plain-Jane property) gets minimal traction online and even less on online travel agencies (OTAs). As traditional houses become more regulated, typical glamping sites have been set up to thrive as commercial campgrounds or vacation rental properties.

The guest avatar is set up for success with constant visits and more minor start-up costs. Couples dominate this market, with smaller families contributing a steady stream of bookings. This allows smaller units (think 200–500 square feet) to outperform larger ones in occupancy rates while costing less to operate and build out. Smaller units near each other on one parcel of land also allow for bigger families to still take part in the glamping adventure and booking multiple structures at once. This dual benefit makes them a favorite among glamping entrepreneurs.

Glamping investors have the ability to find the fine balance between cash-flowing units and equity-enhancing units. Some units that are not typical housing structures (tents, geo domes, etc.) may not hold much equitable value if you plan to sell at any point but do offer lower start-up costs and typically cash flow more than other units that cost more to build.

Units that have more equitable value (cabins, etc.) that are more traditionally built will help build equity into the site as permanent structures. The start-up costs on these are typically much higher and may take longer to cash flow with the amount of money that went into building. Finding a balance between structures is the sweet spot to balance every lever you need to pull when building your glamping site for the most profitable venture possible. We will cover structures more in a later chapter.

Competition Analysis

People have long considered short-term rentals and hotels to be major competitors. While that battle continues, one thing is sure about glamping: Your competition is not hotels. It is essential to be aware of these businesses in your market, but most guests who come to your property never consider a conventional type of accommodation. Glamping exists in a unique sweet spot, offering an experience neither can replicate. Marriott recently (2024) purchased Postcard Cabins, the USA's leading glamping company by volume, with over 1,200 cabins in twenty-nine states.[3] Disney's investment in the new DVC Cabins at Fort Wilderness signals a major vote of confidence in the glamping industry, proving that demand for high-end, nature-based stays is on the rise.[4] Major hotel players see where demographics are shifting and are trying to get on board.

When I first started looking in areas I was interested in, I went on Google and typed in "glamping in X city." This was 2019, so not many popped up at the time. Fast forward to today and typing that phrase in will most likely get starkly different results. This doesn't mean it's oversaturated; it just means you need to know the data inside and out for these different markets.

Evaluating the glamping competition is crucial to get an accurate estimate of what you can make and the chances of permitting issues and if you may be too late to the party in that particular market. Use tools like AirDNA, PriceLabs, or even Airbnb's platform to identify what's already available in your desired area. If you do not see any glamping sites, then you need to ask yourself a few questions.

- Does this market have strong vacation rental data?
- Would you want to travel to this location as a vacation?
- Are there any major metro hubs within one hour?
- Are there any traditional campgrounds at least?

If you do see an active glamping site(s):

- What are their revenue numbers?
- Can you find a glamping niche to fill?
- How saturated is the market for this type of accommodation?

Each scenario has its pros and cons when looking at the available data, assuming that the market has a history of vacation rentals. If there is no active site, your permitting will become more difficult, as you have to be the first to work with the local departments on a project like this. You also don't have genuinely comparable data to

---

[3] "Marriott Acquires the Postcard Cabins Brand: A New Chapter for Outdoor Hospitality," *PR Newswire*, 12 December 2024, https://www.prnewswire.com/news-releases/marriott-acquires-the-postcard-cabins-brand-a-new-chapter-for-outdoor-hospitality-302330192.html.

[4] Michelle Spitzer, "New Disney cabins open at Disney's Fort Wilderness replacing the iconic log ones," *Florida Today*, 2 July 2024, https://www.floridatoday.com/story/news/local/2024/07/01/disneys-fort-wilderness-resort-opens-new-cabins-replacing-log-ones/74267466007/.

back up your revenue estimates. On the other hand, you will be able to dominate that particular market and garner all the demand for unique accommodations. You can establish a brand and quickly become one of the most profitable stays in the market.

If there are active sites in your target area, you will be competing against well-established operators who have already built strong reputations and guest loyalty. To differentiate yourself and attract potential guests, you must compete effectively in several key areas:

- **Price:** Offering competitive pricing or providing better value for the same rate can influence booking decisions. Discounts, package deals, or extended-stay promotions can also help attract more guests.
- **Unique features:** Standing out in the glamping market requires more than just a beautiful location. Whether it's themed accommodations, immersive nature experiences, or high-end design elements, creating a distinctive appeal is essential.
- **Amenities:** Luxury amenities such as hot tubs, private decks, outdoor showers, or on-site activities can make your site more attractive to guests who are looking for a premium experience.

While competition can be a challenge, there are advantages to entering a market with existing glamping operators. Having active competitors means there are proven demand and revenue potential, allowing you to leverage real-world data when forecasting your financials. This eliminates much of the guesswork involved in estimating occupancy rates and pricing strategies. You will be able to analyze why one site outperformed another one and what key details may have made it more successful.

Additionally, navigating local permitting processes can be easier when the authorities are already familiar with the concept of glamping. Existing businesses in the area serve as precedents, reducing the risk of unforeseen regulatory hurdles. Hopefully, the other glamping sites in the area are permitted, and you aren't ringing the alarm to a situation you are potentially entering.

Regardless of the current market situation, uniqueness is key—if your site doesn't stand out, you're in for an uphill battle. Travelers are increasingly drawn to one-of-a-kind experiences, and a generic setup won't generate the buzz or repeat business needed for long-term success. Consider what makes your location, accommodations, and guest experience truly special, and capitalize on those aspects to establish a strong market presence.

Final Thoughts

The best time to get into glamping was ten years ago—the second-best time is now. The experiential hospitality market is growing fast, and even major hotel chains are paying attention. Yes, the competition is tougher, but so is the opportunity. More and more guests are actively seeking these kinds of unique stays.

I'm not here to sugarcoat anything—building my first site was hard work. I spent countless days and nights on it, all while working a full-time job. What got me through was patience, diligence, and staying informed on market shifts. These projects almost always take longer and cost more than expected. But this guide, built on my wins and losses, will save you some serious heartache (and a few bank overdrafts).

Lessons from the Field

- **Glamping is about experience, not just accommodation.** Guests want the beauty of nature with the comforts of a hotel, making design and amenities just as important as location.
- **Know your audience.** The core glamping demographic skews female, millennial, and experience driven, with Gen Z increasingly looking for sustainable and unique travel.
- **Social media fuels demand.** Unique structures get free marketing as guests share their stays online, creating organic buzz that traditional short-term rentals struggle to match.
- **Smaller units maximize returns.** Compact glamping units (200–500 square feet) maintain high occupancy while being cheaper to build and operate, outperforming larger vacation homes.
- **Balance cash flow and equity.** Nontraditional structures like domes and tents generate strong revenue but have little resale value, while permanent builds like cabins boost site equity. A mix of both is ideal.

- **Competition isn't hotels; it's other glamping operators.** Guests seeking a glamping stay rarely compare it to a hotel; they're looking for the most unique and well-designed outdoor experience.
- **Standing out is everything.** If your site isn't unique, it won't succeed. Strong branding, high-end design, and memorable guest experiences separate top-performing glamping.

Chapter 2

Planning Your Glamping Business

The saying "you don't know what you don't know" will come into play more than you think when planning your glamping business. I constantly learned (and am still learning) so many things during my journey that I expect a new surprise every day. Did you know near Austin, Texas, you can't dig for six months of the year because of a Houston toad?

I'm sure you want to conquer the world with your first glamping site, but I stress to you to start small. You should have a vision and plan for your site for the next ten years, but don't expect to be fully built in year one. Let's start with the first baby steps, which is planning your exact glamping business model to eventually hit that ten-year goal.

Choosing a Business Model

Every glamping business is unique, and the options are endless. Every day, there is a new glamping structure on the market, new exclusive amenities that can be added, and markets to explore. Some sites focus on exclusivity, with just a few high-end units spread across acres of land, while others pack in multiple structures to maximize revenue.

One of the best pieces of advice I can give to potential glamprenuers is to visit sites that operate differently. See what sites may have structures you are interested in and a similar market to yours. Study exactly what they are doing right and what you would prefer to be different from your perspective as a guest.

- How is their customer service?
- How easy is it to navigate to their site?
- How was the booking experience?
- What amenities did they offer and you loved?

I've stayed on sites that had eight geo domes side by side, another with twelve yurts spaced on three acres, a high-end site that featured three unique cabins, and off-grid domes in the desert, and have made notes as to which were my favorite and least favorite features. When building my first site, I knew I wanted to create something that incorporated all of my favorite attributes and minimized the least favorite from my visits.

- Should you trade a lower average daily rate (ADR) for more units?
- Will more privacy allow for better revenue?
- What about minimizing operation expenses with fewer units?

Pricing Structure		
Price Level		**Details**
Budget	$50–$100	Typically more units (10–30+) with less amenities (possibly off-grid)
Mid-Tier	$100–$300	Typically more units (5–20+) with average level amenities (indoor bathroom, firepits, electricity)
High-End	$300–$500	Typically average number (3–15) of units with high-end amenities (hot tubs, en suite bathrooms, internet, etc.)
Luxury	$500+	Less units (1–12) with the highest level of amenities possible and high-level vacation rental location (pools, saunas, hot tubs, high-end amenities)

I knew I wanted my first site to feature four to five high-end units on ten acres, offering plenty of privacy. We are one of the highest ADRs in the area, and consistently hit 80–90 percent occupancy rates because I knew people would pay more for privacy. On the other hand, I've seen successful models with ten-plus units on just three acres. These sites can still generate an above-average ADR and run more efficiently on the operation side. More units mean less per-unit expenses and labor costs, and you can spread out your marketing budget over more units. Both approaches work, but they cater to different audiences.

- **ADR vs. scale:** Fewer units with more privacy often command ADRs. However, more units simplify scaling by streamlining operations like cleaning, maintenance, and marketing.
- **Guest experience:** Before deciding on your setup, visit established glamping sites. Stay at both high-density and secluded locations to understand what resonates with guests. I've found that privacy and seclusion often justify higher rates.

Choosing the Right Market (60/30/10 Rule)

As you begin searching for the most promising glamping market at an affordable cost, you might find yourself tempted by cheap, rural land out in the middle of nowhere. I get it—the appeal is real. Lower up-front costs, more relaxed permitting, and the freedom to build something completely your own without a competitor in sight—it sounds like a dream.

But here's the reality check: Without nearby attractions, a major metro within reach, or a reason for people to visit the area, you're facing an uphill battle. There's no built-in demand. You'll be relying entirely on your own destination marketing to get bookings—which is expensive, time-consuming, and rarely scalable for beginners.

And that's just the start. Here are several more reasons to reconsider developing in the middle of nowhere:

- **Operations become a headache.** Cleaners and maintenance crews are tough to find and even harder to keep when the nearest town is an hour away.
- **Materials and supplies take longer to get and cost more**. This adds up fast during the build and beyond.
- **Infrastructure is inconsistent.** Roads, utilities, and emergency access can become major obstacles, especially when trying to deliver a great guest experience.

I almost made this exact mistake.

Early in my search, I found a beautiful, remote piece of land that checked all the emotional boxes—tons of space, wooded acreage, complete privacy. But once I dug into the logistics, it was a clear no-go. It was nearly two hours from the closest major city and an hour from anything even remotely interesting to do. No hiking trails, no lakes, no cute towns—just open land and a long drive to everything.

Had I pulled the trigger, I would've been stuck trying to manufacture demand from scratch, spending more on marketing than I ever planned, and burning out on the operations alone.

That's when I developed the 60/30/10 Rule—a simple framework that's saved me (and many others) from bad investments ever since. Properties that meet this Rule are:

- **60 minutes or less from a major metro** (500,000+ residents).

- **30 minutes or less from a major attraction** (state/national park, lake, mountain, etc.).
- **10 minutes or less from basic civilization** (gas, groceries, restaurants, etc.).

Once I started filtering land through that lens, the difference was night and day. My next property was not only easier to build and run but also booked faster and more consistently, with far less marketing effort. Guests were already coming to the area—I just had to give them a reason to stay with me.

Unless you have an unlimited marketing budget and a multi million-dollar immersive experience, a remote location will likely struggle to attract a steady flow of guests. Instead, follow the 60/30/10 Rule to ensure a sustainable and profitable glamping operation.

60 Minutes from a Metro Hub

Your site should be within an hour's drive of a city with at least 500,000 residents. Ideally, it should sit within a golden triangle of multiple metropolitan areas to maximize exposure to potential guests. My main site is an hour north of Houston, Texas, and within a two-to-three-hour drive of Dallas, Austin, and San Antonio—major cities with growing populations looking for unique, nature-driven experiences. Proximity to these metro areas ensures a steady flow of visitors who can drive in for a weekend getaway without needing to plan an extensive trip.

Guests heavily factor driving distance into their travel decisions. A location too far from a metro area risks losing bookings to closer alternatives, while a spot within an hour's drive can thrive on weekenders and last-minute travelers. This distance also helps with staffing, as employees won't need to commute extreme distances to maintain the site.

30 Minutes from Attractions

Being near state parks, lakes, hiking trails, or other natural landmarks gives guests an additional reason to choose your glamping site. While proximity to national parks can be a strong selling point, state and regional attractions often provide more sustainable, repeat traffic.

NATIONAL ATTRACTIONS VS. STATE/REGIONAL ATTRACTIONS

- National parks attract travelers willing to spend more on their stay, but they also come with stiff competition and often require premium pricing
- State and regional attractions may bring in repeat visitors and shorter trips, leading to consistent year-round bookings
- ADR will vary depending on location, but state/regional attraction areas often have lower competition and start-up costs, making them easier markets to enter
- National parks often come with heavy regulatory requirements, seasonal fluctuations, and sometimes limitations on STR operations due to federal regulations

For example, my glamping site benefits from its proximity to Lake Livingston (Texas's second-largest lake), a national forest, and a state park, ensuring a steady flow of outdoor enthusiasts looking for unique stays. By positioning your site near a mix of attractions, you can appeal to different types of travelers, from hikers and campers to families and weekend adventurers.

10 Minutes from Civilization

Guests want a balance between seclusion and convenience. While they love the idea of escaping the city, they don't want to be completely isolated. Being within ten minutes of a gas station, grocery store, or small town makes their experience more comfortable and your business easier to manage.

From an operational standpoint, this is crucial. The farther you are from essential services, the harder it becomes to:

- Find and retain staff willing to travel long distances for work.
- Keep up with supply runs for toiletries, food, and maintenance materials.
- Provide emergency access to medical care, which some guests may require.
- Maintain high guest satisfaction—even the most adventurous travelers appreciate knowing that they can easily grab essentials if needed.

A balance between remoteness and accessibility ensures your guests feel adventurous without sacrificing convenience. Your workforce, vendors, and support systems will also benefit, making it easier to maintain daily operations.

I wanted to share a few examples of markets that perfectly follow the 60/30/10 Rule—and are now thriving because of it. These areas have quickly emerged as top performers in the glamping space, earning some of the highest short-term rental ratings from AirDNA. Just a few years ago, they weren't even on most investors' radars. But thanks to their ideal mix of accessibility, nearby attractions, and infrastructure, they've become proof of what's possible when a market fits this rule.

Case Study: Fredericksburg, TX

Strategic Location and Accessibility

Fredericksburg is centrally located in Texas Hill Country, making it an ideal getaway for millions of travelers. It's within driving distance of major metro areas, including:

- Greater Houston (7 million+ people): 4 hours away
- Greater Dallas-Fort Worth (8 million+ people): 4 hours away
- Greater Austin (2.5 million+ people): 1 hour away
- Greater San Antonio (2.6 million+ people): 1.5 hours away

With over 20 million-plus potential weekend visitors, the demand for unique stays like glamping is high.

Tourism and Visitor Demand

Fredericksburg attracts 1.5 million+ tourists annually, drawn by its rich German heritage, vibrant wine culture, and outdoor experiences. Known as the "Wine Capital of Texas," the area boasts seventy-plus wineries, making it a top destination for wine tourism. Beyond wine, Enchanted Rock State Park brings in hikers, rock climbers, and nature lovers looking for adventure. This combination of luxury wine experiences and outdoor recreation makes glamping a natural fit for the market.

Market Opportunity for Glamping

The short-term rental market in Fredericksburg is strong, with high ADRs and weekend demand surges due to its popularity as a getaway destination. Unlike major cities where STR regulations are tightening, Fredericksburg's tourism-driven economy is more welcoming to vacation rentals. A prime example of successful glamping sites located here are StayOnera, Spoon Mountain Glamping, etc.

Investing in a glamping site here offers high occupancy potential, strong pricing power, and a unique experience that stands out from traditional hotels and rentals.

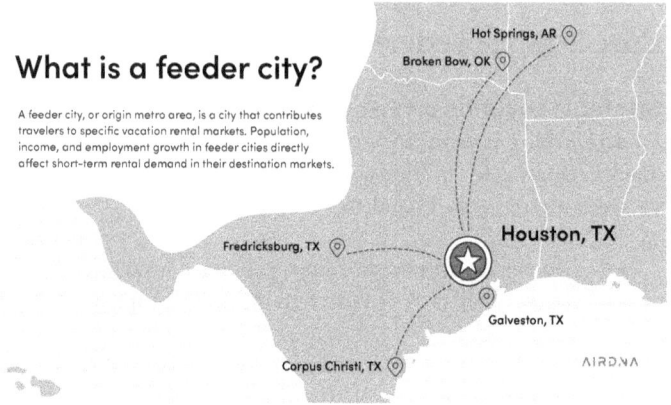

Source: Airdna

Case Study: Asheville, NC

Strategic Location and Accessibility

Asheville sits in the heart of the Blue Ridge Mountains and functions as its own destination city. While it isn't directly next to a major metro like Charlotte, it *is* one of the most visited small cities in the Southeast due to its mix of culture, outdoor adventure, and year-round tourism appeal.

Nearby major metros include:

- Charlotte, NC (2.6 million+ people): 2.25 hours away
- Greenville, SC (950,000+ people): 1 hour away
- Knoxville, TN (870,000+ people): 2 hours away
- Atlanta, GA (6 million+ people): 3.5 hours away

Tourism and Visitor Demand

Asheville welcomes 11 million-plus visitors annually, many of whom come for a mix of food, music, arts, and nature. It's home to the iconic Biltmore Estate, the Blue Ridge Parkway, and Pisgah National Forest—plus a thriving local scene with breweries, farm-to-table dining, and festivals year-round. Asheville's blend of mountain adventure and vibrant culture makes it a magnet for both outdoor lovers and luxury travelers.

This mix makes the market ideal for experiential stays like glamping. Travelers aren't just looking for a place to sleep—they're seeking immersive nature-meets-comfort experiences, and glamping delivers.

Market Opportunity for Glamping

Asheville's short-term rental market remains strong, with consistently high demand, especially on weekends and during fall foliage season. Unlike many cities cracking down on STRs, Asheville and surrounding counties offer more flexibility when operating outside strict city limits. The best examples of successful glamping here are Asheville Glamping, The Glamping Collective, and more.

Glamping properties near Asheville benefit from:

- Year-round tourism (fall foliage, winter cabins, spring hikes, summer road trips).
- High nightly rates due to luxury demand.
- Guests actively seeking nature and comfort hybrid stays.

For investors, the opportunity lies in creating a standout property that taps into Asheville's outdoorsy-meets-artsy vibe—think A-frames in the trees, geodesic domes with mountain views, or yurts near waterfall trails. The region's tourism infrastructure, deep visitor base, and natural beauty make it a prime market to build in.

While the 60/30/10 Rule provides a strong foundation for location selection, there are additional factors to consider to ensure long-term success.

- **Seasonality:** Some regions experience extreme weather fluctuations that may limit year-round occupancy. Consider whether your site will need adjustments for off-season operations, such as heating for winter guests or cooling solutions for hot summers.
- **Local Regulations and zoning:** Research local STR regulations, zoning laws, and environmental policies. Some areas impose strict limitations on STRs, while others are more welcoming to ecotourism developments.
- **Competition and demand analysis:** Look at existing glamping sites in your target market. If there are too many, differentiation is key. If there are none, determine if the lack of competition is due to demand issues rather than untapped opportunity.
- **Infrastructure and utilities:** Consider access to water, electricity, and reliable internet, as these are crucial to guest satisfaction. Off-grid locations may require additional investment in solar power, septic systems, and water filtration.

By following the 60/30/10 Rule and carefully evaluating market conditions, you can set yourself up for higher occupancy, reduced operational struggles, and long-term profitability in the growing glamping market. While it may be tempting to buy cheap land and assume that demand will follow, strategic location selection is the single most important factor in ensuring your glamping business thrives. Some things are cheap for a reason.

Glamping is not just about offering unique accommodations; it's about creating an accessible, well-positioned experience that aligns with travel demand and convenience. If you prioritize market research, accessibility, and differentiation, your site has a much greater chance of sustained success and high profitability.

Understanding Local Regulations

Start by understanding your local regulations. Counties and cities often have different requirements, so it's crucial to establish clear communication with officials early on. A great starting point is to search online for the local county permitting department's contact information and reach out directly. However, you'll need to have a basic game plan before reaching out to receive helpful guidance.

Here are a few key questions to answer before speaking with officials:

- What type of structures do you want to build?
- How many units are you considering?
- What type of septic or waste management system will you have?
- What are your operation plans (seasonal or year-round)?
- What are your security and emergency plans?

The more clarity you have on your project scope, the better response you will receive from the county. If you approach them without a clear concept, you risk being dismissed or met with excessive resistance. A majority of small-town areas have smaller departments, and may even have just one or two people who handle the permitting process. Your chances of success increase in relation to the amount of preparation you do in understanding your vision fully.

Permitting can be one of the biggest hurdles, but it's not insurmountable. Most locations are familiar with campgrounds and have a history of vacation rentals, if you are looking in the correct markets. The hardest part is getting the actual structures compliant with the local regulations. Glamping structures generally fall into two categories:

- **Nonpermanent structures:** These include tents, yurts, domes, and other units that aren't fixed to a foundation. This also can include anything with wheels and a chassis attached to it. They're often easier to permit as campgrounds or RV park models.
- **Permanent structures:** Cabins, tree houses, shipping containers, and other units tied to permanent foundations require more rigorous permitting for utilities and zoning.

ÖÖD Mirror House www.oodhouse.com

If you are planning for permanent structures, ensure that the structure type has architectural plans that comply with local building codes. Some budget-friendly options may lack the necessary documentation, making it nearly impossible to get them approved. When possible, choose structures that have stamped architectural and engineering plans to expedite the approval process. As glamping is evolving, there are several structures now being made that have the ability to produce these plans in-house.

Counties and municipalities often have strict building codes, especially regarding utilities, foundations, and structural integrity. Some zoning departments may also require ADA compliance, fire suppression systems, or stormwater management plans. Knowing what your local government expects up front can save you time and headaches down the road.

One of the most significant concerns for county approval is the septic and waste management system. A ten-unit glamping site will require a much larger septic system than a three-unit site, and the permitting process will vary depending on the number of units and the county's environmental regulations. You will most likely need a commercial septic system, but this is one utility that is very critical to consider in terms of your long-term goals.

Here are key factors to consider:

- **Type of waste system:** Will each unit have a private bathroom, or will there be a shared bathhouse? Some counties require one septic system per acre while others allow shared systems. Each county has specific requirements for this and talking with reputable and licensed local septic companies can help give you some clarity.
- **Engineering and approval:** Septic systems must be designed by a licensed sanitation engineer and approved by the county before construction can begin. I highly recommend leaning on qualified companies here to understand the inner workings and criteria. This is typically the biggest reason projects will be not permitted, along with structural integrity.
- **Alternative waste solutions:** If standard septic is not an option, composting toilets, gray water systems, or off-grid solutions may be viable, but these require additional county approvals. Remember that these typically bring in a much lower ADR from guests, and cleaners will not be a fan of this method. I do not recommend this but do understand there are successful glamping sites that use these systems.
- **Drainage and soil considerations:** Some counties conduct percolation tests to determine whether the land is suitable for traditional septic systems. If the soil doesn't drain well, you may have to explore alternative waste disposal options.

Understanding these requirements early on will help avoid costly redesigns or, worse, investing in land that isn't suitable for development. Lean on others who are more experienced in this field to make sure you prepare properly.

Approaching local officials with a structured plan increases your chances of receiving guidance and approvals. Simply calling and saying, "Hey, I would like to start a glamping site" won't yield productive results. Instead, present a phased development plan that shows responsible growth and environmental considerations.

If county officials have never dealt with glamping projects before, expect many questions along the lines of "Glamping? What on earth is that?" Some counties will be welcoming and open to discussion while others may immediately reject the concept. If you receive an immediate "absolutely not," it may be best to look for another location with more flexible regulations. If you receive a "maybe" or "here's how to submit a proposal," you've found a potential market that is worth exploring further.

Some counties require conditional use permits (CUPs) or special-use permits (SUPs) for glamping operations. Being patient and flexible throughout this process is key, as some approvals can take months.

Your chances of obtaining permits increase if there are currently active glamping sites or unique builds in the area. A simple google search, scroll on Airbnb in your market, and search on social media will give you clear insight into whether any existing operators have launched a site successfully in the area. If these structures were legally permitted, they serve as a precedent when presenting your case to zoning officials.

To streamline your research:

- Ask the county for a zoning map that shows unrestricted, commercial, and special-use areas to help narrow down your search.
- Request information about similar approved businesses in the area to gauge how flexible or restrictive local officials are.
- If permitted glamping sites exist, visit them to see how they operate and how they may have navigated local zoning challenges. You should only do this with permission from the owner or, the ultimate reconnaissance, booking a stay.

Understanding the regulatory landscape before you buy land or start construction can save time, money, and frustration. While permitting can seem like a daunting hurdle, the right approach—early planning, structured communication, and alignment with local requirements—can help ensure your glamping project gets the green light.

Pro Tips

Call a few local contractors or home builders you may be interested in working with. During your initial conversations, ask if they have experience with permits in different local counties. Contractors who regularly work in the area will have firsthand knowledge of the challenges involved in permitting and can provide valuable insights into the regulatory climate of each jurisdiction.

I strongly considered two neighboring counties during my first purchase and could not decide which would be easier after talking with both. I asked some contractors for their opinions on my chances with each. Both responded, "County X is a nightmare to deal with; County Y is much more understanding," which instantly told me where I needed to focus. This type of feedback can be invaluable, as it saves you time and effort that might otherwise be wasted on an overly restrictive county.

Additionally, contractors can provide guidance on estimated build costs, local material availability, and potential challenges that could affect your construction timeline. They may also have established relationships with county permitting offices, making the process smoother for your project.

This is also when working with a trusted real estate agent who knows the area's short-term rental market and zoning requirements becomes invaluable. A knowledgeable agent can help you navigate different locations, identify properties that align with your business goals, and provide insight into which counties or municipalities are more favorable toward short-term rentals and glamping developments. They typically have access to more back-end information and a more extensive network to help you find the ideal location for smooth approval.

A good real estate agent can connect you with property owners who may already have land that meets zoning requirements or with investors who have successfully launched similar projects in the area.

Their connections can also lead to introductions with local attorneys, surveyors, and planners who specialize in navigating land-use and permitting regulations.

By leveraging both contractor and real estate agent expertise, you can avoid costly mistakes, streamline the approval process, and position yourself in a location where you are set up for success from the start.

Final Thoughts

Planning your glamping business isn't just about dreaming up beautiful structures—it's about building something that works, lasts, and scales. It's about knowing when to start small, when to expand, and how to adapt when the rules change or the unexpected shows up (like a Houston toad halting your dig for half the year).

If I've learned anything in this journey, it's this: The best glamping operators are flexible, strategic, and obsessed with getting the fundamentals right. That means choosing the right market, understanding your guest, knowing your zoning, and building with intention—not impulse.

You don't need to conquer the world on day one. You need a solid foundation—both literally and figuratively. Everything else comes after that.

Lessons from the Field

- **Start small, think big.** Dream about your ten-year plan, but build for year one. Scaling too fast can burn you out before your business gets momentum.
- **Visit other sites.** Before building, I visited multiple glamping sites—domes, yurts, off-grid cabins—and took detailed notes. Seeing what worked (and what didn't) from a guest's POV was priceless.
- **More privacy, higher rates.** My four high-end units on ten acres earn one of the highest ADRs in the region. Guests will pay for space, quiet, and exclusivity.
- **More units, more efficiency.** I've seen sites crush it with ten-plus units on just three acres. With smart design, scale can mean higher total revenue and lower per-unit costs.

- **Don't be fooled by cheap land.** If your property isn't near a metro, attraction, or civilization, expect to do all the heavy lifting on demand—and operations will be a nightmare.
- **Use the 60/30/10 Rule.** This framework saved me from investing in remote land that looked perfect on paper but would've been a logistical mess.
- **Infrastructure will make or break you.** Septic, water, electric, and road access aren't exciting—but they're mission-critical. Plan for the boring stuff first.
- **Regulations matter (a lot).** Don't buy until you've talked to the county. The right approach, with clear plans and a phased vision, can open more doors than you think.
- **Permanent vs. nonpermanent builds.** Know what your county prefers before choosing your structure. A beautiful tiny home without proper documentation is a permit killer.

Chapter 3

Finding a Glamping Property

Once I finally identified a winning market, I knew the hard part wasn't over—it was just beginning. Finding the *right* property in that market felt overwhelming at first. I hit the ground running, touring every listing with acreage I could find. But pretty quickly, I realized I was just spinning my wheels.

The problem? I didn't yet know exactly what I was looking for.

That clarity came with time. I learned I needed more land than I initially expected. I started paying attention to things like road conditions—some properties had access roads so bad they were practically unusable. I even learned to check if there were garbage dumps or industrial sites nearby that could kill the vibe for future guests.

This process wasn't quick. It took eight months and multiple trips to the area to finally feel confident in what I needed and where I wanted to be.

Here's my advice: Be ready to put in the reps. Explore. Drive the back roads. Talk to neighbors. Look beyond the listing photos. The more you immerse yourself in the area, the more equipped you'll be to spot the perfect opportunity when it comes.

Be patient, dig into the next section, and you'll save yourself a ton of wasted time—and maybe even land the kind of property that changes everything.

Property Sourcing Strategies

Unfortunately, no MLS (Multiple Listing Service) specifically exists for glamping properties. However, potential investors can use a few strategies to find the perfect property to start their glamping business. Here are some tips and tricks I've used and others can utilize.

Real Estate Agents

One of the best ways to source glamping properties is by working with real estate agents who understand the market or area you're targeting and know how short-term rentals work. Remember that being a short-term rental specialist isn't taught in real estate school; it's learned through experience in this niche.

Real estate agents can be invaluable when sourcing glamping properties. Look for agents who specialize in rural or recreational land sales. Ask about their experience with properties suited for unique stays and whether they understand the zoning and permitting challenges related to glamping.

Here are three key questions to ask every real estate agent you interview:

1. Do you own any short-term rentals?
2. How many short-term-rental-related sales have you completed in the past twelve months?
3. Do you have connections to property management, cleaners, maintenance teams, and subcontractors?

If the answers to these questions are mostly no, it might be a sign to look elsewhere. Luckily, BiggerPockets offers an Investor-Friendly Real Estate Agent Finder to help you find STR-specific agents in your desired market (www.BiggerPockets.com/BookAgent).

Pro Tip: Build relationships with agents who do a lot of deals in your target area. These agents will likely know about off-market deals, as many rural properties never even hit mainstream listings. Having a connected agent is crucial.

Direct-to-Owner Strategy

Reaching out directly to landowners can uncover hidden gems. Use platforms like PropStream or county records to find owners of underutilized land or properties. Personalized letters, postcards, or even cold calls can help initiate conversations. A real estate agent can also help source information for you locally if they have access to the MLS.

This strategy requires more effort and has a lower success rate than others, but it can lead to finding the best deals. For example, if you spot land listed online through platforms like Zillow by owner, there's a higher chance you might be able to negotiate an owner-direct deal.

Land Auctions and Foreclosures

Land auctions, foreclosure sales, and tax lien properties often provide opportunities to acquire land below market value. However, these deals require thorough research and a clear understanding of auction terms.

- Always perform due diligence before bidding
- Auctions often have "as-is" clauses, including environmental or zoning issues
- Many auctions require cash purchases

Converting Existing Campgrounds or Resorts

This may be my favorite approach for many reasons. Existing campgrounds, RV parks, or small resorts can offer ready-made infrastructure, such as utilities, parking, and established guest amenities like bathhouses, roads, and waste management systems. Instead of starting from scratch, you can leverage existing infrastructure to transform the site into a high-end glamping destination, saving both time and capital while reducing the complexities of permitting and development.

Additionally, many of these properties are mom-and-pop operations, meaning they have been managed by the same owners for decades. Often, these owners are nearing retirement and looking for a viable exit strategy, creating a prime opportunity for investors seeking a win-win acquisition. The likelihood of seller financing is much higher in these cases, as many owners would prefer to finance the deal themselves rather than waiting for a traditional buyer. This not only reduces your up-front capital investment but also provides flexible terms that can support your business's early cash flow.

Beyond the financial benefits, existing operations typically have an established customer base that can generate immediate revenue. Whether it's seasonal visitors, RV travelers, or vacationing families, converting an operational campground into a glamping site allows you to tap into existing demand while rebranding for a higher-end market.

The key to success in this strategy is evaluating underperforming sites that have strong potential for repositioning. Properties that have been neglected or have minimal modern amenities often present the best opportunities for transformation. By implementing unique glamping accommodations, enhancing the guest experience, and upgrading marketing efforts, you can revitalize a site and significantly increase revenue.

Many of these properties do not typically sell quickly online, meaning there's less competition compared to traditional investment properties. Many deals can be found off-market or through direct outreach to owners, allowing for more favorable negotiations.

Ultimately, acquiring an existing campground or small resort offers a rare combination of immediate income, infrastructure savings, and high-value repositioning potential. For investors looking to scale efficiently, this strategy provides an excellent way to enter the glamping market with fewer start-up challenges and built-in operational advantages.

How to Find These Properties

There are two ways to find these properties: searching online using terms like "[Market Name] campground" or "[Market Name] RV park" or looking for properties that appear outdated or poorly maintained. These are often owned by individuals who might be ready to sell.

Evaluate the property's current guest base and amenities to understand its existing strengths and areas for improvement. Identify the type of guests who frequent the site—are they weekend campers, RV travelers, families, or adventure seekers? Understanding their current audience will help determine how best to position and enhance the property.

Consider if you can elevate the guest experience by adding unique glamping units that cater to a higher-end market. This could include luxury tents, geodesic domes, tree houses, or tiny cabins with modern amenities. The goal is to create an experience that stands out, enticing a new segment of travelers who are looking for something beyond traditional camping.

Beyond accommodations, assess the existing amenities and determine how they can be upgraded or expanded. Enhancements like private outdoor soaking tubs, communal firepits, farm-to-table dining experiences, or guided adventure excursions can significantly increase a property's appeal. Upgrading utilities, adding high-speed Wi-Fi, or creating dedicated workspaces can also attract remote workers and digital nomads who seek longer stays.

Evaluating the property's guest base and amenities should guide a strategic investment plan that maximizes revenue potential and differentiates your site in the competitive glamping market.

Commercial Real Estate Websites

Websites like LoopNet, Crexi, and LandWatch are excellent tools for finding land suitable for glamping. These platforms specialize in commercial, recreational, and raw land listings, making them a great starting point for investors looking to develop a unique short-term rental property.

To avoid endlessly scrolling through listings, set up custom alerts with key filters such as acreage, zoning, proximity to attractions, and utilities. The land should be large enough to accommodate your glamping setup, whether that's multiple units or a single high-end structure. Zoning is crucial since some rural or agricultural areas allow for glamping, but it's important to confirm local ordinances to avoid unexpected roadblocks.

Land listed on LoopNet and Crexi is often marketed by brokers who recognize its development potential, which means prices may be higher than off-market opportunities. While these listings can still be great investments, it's important to analyze the numbers carefully. Running projections for average daily rates, occupancy rates, and development costs will help determine whether a deal makes financial sense. Avoid overpaying based on emotion—scenic land might seem like a dream, but an overpriced deal can quickly erode profitability.

A smart strategy is to target expired or stale listings. If a property has been sitting for months, the seller may be open to negotiating a lower price. Reaching out with an offer below asking could result in a deal that brokers didn't anticipate.

Networking with Local Experts

Beyond agents and online tools, tap into local networks like community boards, business organizations, and tourism offices. Local experts often have insider knowledge of properties that haven't been widely advertised. Building relationships with people in the community can open doors to opportunities you might not find elsewhere.

- Go to local real estate meet ups
- Engage in the BiggerPockets Forums and Facebook Groups (www.BiggerPockets.com/BookSTRForums)
- Join glamping-specific Facebook Groups
- Attend real estate conferences like BPCON (www.BiggerPockets.com/BookBPCON)

All of these ideas and others that can lead to networking with the right individuals just take patience and putting yourself out there. It may seem empowering to do it all yourself, but in reality, the more expertise you have around you, the higher your chances are of being successful.

Deal Evaluation

You may come across what seems like the perfect property—but without accurate revenue projections, you could fall behind before you even start. The first step in evaluating any glamping investment is understanding what it can realistically earn.

Start with Market Research: Airbnb and AirDNA

Before making any investment, analyze local competition to determine pricing trends, occupancy rates, and guest demand. Here's how:

1. Search Airbnb for unique stays in your area
   - Look up comparable properties—geodesic domes, cabins, yurts, or other glamping setups within thirty to fifty miles of your target location.
   - Take notes on:
     - Nightly rates: What do they charge on weekends vs. weekdays?
     - Cleaning fees: This helps estimate an expense you'll need to factor in
     - Review volume: How many reviews do top-performing listings get per month? A property with five-plus reviews per month is likely booking frequently.
     - Calendar availability: Are they booked solid, or do they have open dates? This gives clues about demand and pricing power.

2. Verify data with AirDNA
   - Use AirDNA to pull hard data on average daily rates (ADR), occupancy rates, and annual revenue estimates for glamping stays in your area
   - Key metrics to focus on:
     - Target occupancy rate: The percentage of nights similar properties are booked
     - Average daily rate (ADR): The typical nightly rate you can expect

- Seasonality trends: Are bookings steady year-round, or is there a clear off season?
  - This will help you forecast potential income and adjust projections based on different pricing strategies

Once you have your market data, test different revenue scenarios in your pro forma.

- Adjust unit numbers to see how adding or removing structures affects profitability
- Factor in cleaning fees, maintenance costs, and potential management expenses
- Explore peak season vs. off-season pricing to account for revenue fluctuations

Understanding your revenue potential is critical when seeking funding. The way lenders evaluate your property depends on the type of financing you pursue.

RESIDENTIAL FINANCING

- Residential lenders use the comparable sales approach—they don't care how much the property can make as an STR
- They'll base the loan amount on what similar properties have sold for, not projected rental income
- If using a residential loan, focus on properties that have strong resale value and match what appraisers can compare

COMMERCIAL LOANS AND PRIVATE INVESTORS

- Commercial lenders and investors use the income-based approach—they want to see revenue projections and proof of demand
- They'll expect a full business plan showing projected revenue, expenses, and cash flow
- Having AirDNA data, local STR comps, and a solid pro forma will be key in securing funding

Due Diligence Checklist

The first step in choosing a glamping property isn't just finding a beautiful piece of land—it's running the numbers to see if it will actually cash flow. Use market data, test different scenarios, and align your financial plan with the right financing strategy. Whether you're going for a land-hack strategy with a residential mortgage or pitching investors for a high-end glamping retreat, understanding how your property is valued will set you up for success.

- Verify property boundaries and legal descriptions. Conduct an initial search and obtain a professional survey once under contract.
- Confirm zoning classifications and permitted uses. Double-check with the local county to ensure compliance.
- Assess accessibility and road conditions. Roads requiring four-wheel drive can limit your guest pool.
- Investigate past land use to uncover potential liabilities.

We went in-depth into zoning and permitting in the last chapter, but it would not make sense to discuss development and skip over how significant this portion is again. Once you have identified an address, contact local planning offices to confirm whether the property can legally operate as a glamping site. Check for additional permitting requirements and limits on the number of units or guests.

An environmental assessment is county/city specific; not all will require this type of assessment. Talk with your local permitting department to see if they require this when building and developing your land. You may need to conduct a Phase 1 Environmental Site Assessment to identify potential contamination or hazards. This is particularly important for properties with previous industrial or agricultural use. Remediation can be costly and may restrict land use.

Access issues will be an instant deterrent for potential guests. I have seen many sites with language such as "must have four-wheel drive vehicle" or "high-clearance vehicles only." These properties may have fantastic views and locations, but you are drastically reducing your guest pool. If guests need to rent a truck to get to your property, their expenses will increase, and your occupancy rates will suffer.

Ensure the property's access points are safe and convenient. Guests expect easy entry, adequate parking, and well-maintained roads. Additionally, proximity to hiking trails, lakes, or other natural attractions can significantly enhance a property's value and appeal.

A friend of mine found a perfect property—great views, a great price, and an ideal location. However, after consulting with the county and septic engineers, they learned they could only install five units instead of the ten they had planned. He spent over $3,000 in initial soil tests and consultations only to discover that this deal was no longer viable for the projections he had anticipated.

Now he was out time and money, but he was able to stop a massive disaster before it happened by closing on the property. Confirm these details early to avoid surprises and putting up money that does not need to be spent initially.

Final Thoughts

Finding land for your glamping business is a lot more than scrolling listings and dreaming big. It's a hands-on, patience-testing process that rewards preparation and punishes shortcuts.

I thought the hard part was finding the right market—turns out, sourcing the *right* property within that market was just as tough. I wasted time looking at places that were too remote, too rugged, or too close to unwanted neighbors (think: industrial yards and sketchy access roads). But that process gave me clarity. I started to understand what mattered: good access, infrastructure potential, zoning, guest appeal—and how all of those tie into long-term profitability.

The perfect property isn't just pretty—it's practical. It's buildable. It's legal. And it's aligned with your long-term vision. So don't rush it. Put in the reps. Call the county. Talk to neighbors. Tour properties in person. It may take months, but the right piece of land can become the foundation of a business that changes your life.

Lessons from the Field

- **Remote ≠ profitable.** Cheap, off-grid land may look appealing, but if it's too far from attractions, amenities, or civilization, your bookings (and operations) will suffer.
- **Roads matter. A lot.** Bad access roads kill bookings. If guests need four-wheel drive to reach your site, your occupancy rate will take a hit.
- **Visit in person.** Listing photos won't show you the trash dump next door or the steep, rutted road. Walk the land. Drive the roads. Smell the air.
- **Network relentlessly.** Attend meetups. Post in forums. Go to conferences. The more conversations you have, the more off-market deals and insights you'll uncover.

- **Convert, don't just build.** Buying a struggling RV park or campground can give you instant infrastructure, utilities, and an easier path to profitability than raw land.
- **Zoning isn't optional.** Always check with the county before making an offer. Know the rules for your structure type, guest count, and septic system.
- **Evaluate like an investor, not a dreamer.** Use tools like AirDNA, Airbnb comps, and pricing models to run projections before you get emotionally attached to any property.

Chapter 4

Funding Your Glamping Site

The struggle all glampreneurs face is how they can finance these types of unique business ventures. Cash will always reign supreme in this field, but there are some clever ways to get your glamping business off the ground. I didn't have much when I started, but I was able to sell those three condos I mentioned earlier and go all in on glamping. I was able to get about $40,000 profit from all three to use and had some of my own personal savings (about $50,000) to get started. In this chapter, I'll share some methods that I used for financing the rest of my projects that you can use to finance yours.

Funding Options Chart: List of Pros and Cons	
✅ PROS	➖ CONS
Traditional Bank Loans	
Lower interest rates, structured repayment terms, can build business credit	Strict approval requirements, requires strong credit and financials, collateral needed
SBA Loans	
Lower down payments, longer repayment terms, backed by the government	Lengthy approval process, extensive documentation, must meet SBA requirements
Private Equity Partnerships	
Access to large capital, expert business guidance, rapid scaling potential	Gives up ownership and control, investor expectations and pressure
Private Loans as Debt	
Retain full ownership, flexible repayment terms, no equity dilution	Difficult to obtain without a proven business model, may have high interest rates
Seller Financing	
Low or no down payment, easier approval process, flexible terms	Seller may charge higher interest, limited availability, terms vary widely
Crowdfunding	
No repayment required, potential for high fundraising amounts, broad exposure	Success is not guaranteed, time consuming, platform fees may apply

✅ PROS	⊖ CONS
Grants and Incentives	
No repayment required, can cover significant costs, government or private sources	Highly competitive, strict eligibility requirements, application process can be complex
Cash	
No interest or repayment, full ownership retention, fastest way to close a deal	Requires having enough savings, opportunity cost of tying up liquid assets

Traditional Bank Loans

Conventional loans work well for properties with existing infrastructure and clear revenue potential. Lenders are typically more comfortable financing properties that follow traditional construction models, such as stick-built homes or preapproved developments. To secure funding, be prepared to present a strong business plan, financial projections, and market research to demonstrate viability. However, traditional loans often do not cover unique builds like yurts, domes, or tiny homes, as these structures may not meet conventional lending requirements.

If you're utilizing the land-hacking model, where you start small and develop in phases, a conventional loan can help finance land purchases or initial infrastructure improvements before scaling with alternative funding. This is essentially how I got my start. I found a piece of land with a house on it, used a low-down-payment, owner-occupied loan, and saved the cash to start building my cabins.

SBA Loans

The Small Business Administration (SBA) offers loans specifically for development and tourism-related ventures, making them a strong option for financing glamping projects. SBA loans can cover land acquisition, infrastructure improvements, and construction but require extensive documentation, including detailed financial statements and a proven track record of business success. These loans tend to have longer approval timelines, so they are best suited for investors with a well-structured, long-term development plan.

USDA Loans

The U.S. Department of Agriculture (USDA) offers loans designed to promote rural development, making them an excellent option for financing glamping projects in eligible areas. USDA Business and Industry (B&I) loans can fund land purchases, construction, infrastructure improvements, and working capital. These loans offer low-interest rates and long repayment terms, but they require the project to be located in a rural-designated area and demonstrate economic benefits to the community. While the application process can be extensive, USDA loans are ideal for investors looking to develop sustainable, experience-driven stays in rural markets.

Private Equity Partnerships and Private Loans

For investors looking to scale quickly or launch a high-end glamping resort, private equity partnerships can provide substantial funding. These partnerships involve working with high-net-worth individuals or investment firms that contribute capital in exchange for equity or a share of the profits. While private equity is often associated with people in suits behind glass desks, it doesn't always come from institutional investors—it can also come from friends, family, or private individuals looking to diversify their investments. The key to attracting private equity is presenting a compelling business case that highlights revenue potential, industry growth, and a clear return on investment. This strategy is particularly useful for large-scale glamping projects but does come with trade-offs, as investors will typically require a percentage of ownership and decision-making power in exchange for their capital.

For those who prefer to retain full ownership, private loans offer an alternative route. Instead of exchanging equity for money, private loans involve structured debt financing, where an investor or lender provides capital that must be repaid over time, often with interest. Private loans are one of the most advantageous financing options for glamping site owners because they allow the business to scale without diluting ownership, but they can also be one of the hardest to secure without a proven model or track record of success. Like private equity, these loans can come from friends, family, or private investors, but they can also be sourced from alternative lending companies such as BestEgg, SoFi, and others, which offer personal loans based on factors like creditworthiness rather than requiring collateral. These loans typically range from $10,000 to $75,000, making them a viable option for smaller projects or initial start-up costs.

While both private equity and private loans provide significant advantages, they require careful consideration based on the scale of your glamping business, your risk tolerance, and your long-term ownership goals. Whether working with outside investors or securing debt financing, having a solid business plan and clear financial projections is essential to securing the best funding terms.

Seller Financing

Seller financing is one of the most flexible ways to acquire a property with lower up-front costs and less reliance on traditional banks. Many existing campgrounds, RV parks, and underperforming resorts are owned by individuals looking to exit the business. These owners may be willing to finance the sale themselves, allowing for negotiable down payments, extended repayment terms, and reduced credit requirements. This method is especially useful when purchasing properties that may not qualify for conventional loans due to their unique structures or zoning restrictions.

Crowdfunding Platforms

Crowdfunding allows you to raise capital from multiple investors, either through equity-based crowdfunding or reward-based platforms. Sites like Fundrise, GoFundMe, and IndieGoGo work well when you have a unique concept that can generate excitement among potential investors. This option requires a strong marketing strategy and compelling storytelling to attract backers.

Grants and Incentives

Many local, state, and federal programs offer grants, tax incentives, and subsidies for ecotourism, rural development, and sustainable lodging projects. These programs can significantly reduce up-front costs and improve your return on investment. Examples include:

- State tourism incentives that encourage hospitality growth in designated tourism zones.
- Green energy grants for solar power, water conservation, or other eco-friendly initiatives.

Grants require research and application efforts, but they can provide free capital with no repayment obligations, making them an excellent option for long-term financial sustainability.

Cash

Using cash remains the fastest and simplest way to develop a glamping site. If you have savings or liquid capital, starting with one or two units without relying on lenders eliminates interest payments and financial restrictions. If you plan to self-fund, consider focusing on a structure that holds equitable value, such as a cabin or tiny home, which will make it easier to refinance into a traditional loan later.

One effective strategy is to fund the first build in cash, establish profitability, and then refinance to pull equity out for future expansion. This approach allows you to start generating revenue quickly while setting yourself up for scalable growth without taking on excessive debt up front.

By leveraging multiple funding sources strategically, you can optimize both short-term flexibility and long-term financial stability. Whether you pursue conventional financing, creative seller deals, or alternative capital sources, the key is aligning your funding strategy with your investment goals and market opportunities.

What Is Land Hacking?

Land hacking is the process of purchasing a house with land using a mortgage, then leveraging that land to create a cash-flowing glamping business. Instead of struggling to finance raw land—which is much harder to get a loan for—you buy a home with property, ensuring access to utilities and easier financing. Then, over time, you develop the land into an income-generating site by adding glamping units, tiny homes, cabins, or other unique stays.

Why Land Hacking Works

- **Easier financing:** Banks are much more willing to give you a loan for a house with land than for vacant land alone. Mortgages on raw land often require large down payments, higher interest rates, and strict lending terms. But if there's a livable house on the property, you can take advantage of traditional home loan options.

- **Built-in utilities:** When you buy a house, you're buying access to water, electricity, and septic. These are some of the most expensive and difficult parts of developing raw land. By choosing a home with acreage, you know that these essential services are already in place or at least nearby.
- **Low-Down-Payment Options:**
  - **Owner-occupied loan (5 percent down):** If you plan to live in the home for at least a year, you can take advantage of an owner-occupied conventional or FHA loan with as little as 5 percent down. This keeps your initial investment low and allows you to put more money into building out your glamping business.
  - **Vacation home loan (10 percent down):** If you're buying the property as a second home, you may be eligible for a vacation home loan, with just 10 percent down. However, there are additional requirements, such as the home needing to be a certain distance from your primary residence and being used as a personal getaway when not rented out.
- **Immediate equity growth:** As soon as you add additional rental units—whether it's a yurt, a tiny house, or a high-end glamping tent—you increase the property's value. Not only do you gain additional income streams, but you also start building equity in the property much faster than a traditional homeowner would.

Step-by-Step Guide to Land Hacking for Glamping

1. **Find a house with land**
   - Look for properties with at least a few acres, ideally in an area that allows short-term rentals
   - Prioritize homes that need some work but have beautiful, usable land
   - Check zoning laws to ensure you can legally add rental units
2. **Choose the right loan**
   - Decide if you'll use an owner-occupied loan (live in the house for a year) or a vacation home loan

- Work with a lender familiar with short-term rental financing
3. **Use savings to develop the property**
    - The money saved from a low down payment can be used to fund your first glamping unit
    - Consider starting small with one or two units before scaling up
4. **Start renting and scaling**
    - Once your first glamping unit is up and running, reinvest the profits into adding more
    - Use smart marketing to drive occupancy and maximize revenue
5. **Leverage your equity for expansion**
    - As your property value increases, you can pull equity out through refinancing or a home equity line of credit (HELOC) to fund further expansion

Land hacking is the ultimate shortcut to owning a profitable glamping site without the massive up-front costs of buying and developing raw land from scratch. By purchasing a home with land using a low-down-payment mortgage, you not only secure a place to live but also create an opportunity to build a cash-flowing business.

This strategy allows you to get started in the glamping space with minimal risk and maximum reward. As I mentioned earlier, this exact strategy is how I got my start—and how I took a piece of land valued at $550,000 and turned it into a property now worth over $1.3 million.

It began with finding a solid "good bones" house that needed cosmetic updates. The real value? It sat on eleven acres of prime land, with beautiful views and dense forestry—ideal for future glamping expansion.

I used a 5 percent down owner-occupied loan, putting just $22,500 down. My monthly mortgage came out to about $3,000, and per the loan requirements, I lived on-site for a year. During that time, I used my remaining savings to build my first geo dome, complete with full utilities and infrastructure designed to support additional units later. I also invested in high-ROI renovations to the main house—upgrading the kitchen and bathrooms.

Glamping does require some up-front capital, no matter how you slice it. I had saved about $75,000, which was no small feat. To cover the remaining $50,000 I needed, I tapped into a HELOC on my primary residence. It was a risk, no doubt—but sometimes, that's where the opportunity lies.

That first geo dome alone brought in $8,000 per month, which not only covered the mortgage—it produced cash flow. Once I moved out, I also started renting the main house for another $5,000 per month.

The renovations added $75,000 in equity for a $30,000 spend. And while the dome itself didn't increase the appraisal much, the infrastructure, business income, and scalability added serious value to the overall property. If I ever decide to sell, it's now positioned as a turnkey short-term rental business.

That initial $125,000 investment paid off quickly—and more importantly, it gave me the foundation to add more units, just like I had planned from the start. But how can you exactly get creative to fund your deals?

Here are several examples of land hacking strategies specifically tailored for STR investors.

Parcel and Build Strategy

- **How it works:** Purchase a five-to-ten-acre parcel outside city limits (preferably unrestricted land). Subdivide into two to four parcels.
- **STR angle:** Build one STR on each lot—or live on one and rent the others
- **Example:** Buy ten acres for $200,000 → Split into four 2.5-acre lots → Build four small A-frames or tiny homes, each grossing $40,000/year

Upside: Equity from parceling + STR income
Bonus: Sell one parcel to recoup capital

Anchor Property + Add Units Strategy

- **How it works:** Buy a property with enough land to add structures—like domes, safari tents, tiny houses, or RV pads
- **STR angle:** Launch one unit, reinvest earnings to slowly scale more units on the same land
- **Example:** Start with a $300,000 cabin on four acres → Add a dome year two → Add a container home year three

Upside: Less capital needed up front
Bonus: Shared amenities = higher guest satisfaction

RV/Glamping Flex Zoning Strategy

- **How it works:** Buy raw land in a county with minimal permitting/zoning restrictions. Add off-grid or semi-permitted units like RVs, yurts, or bell tents.
- **STR angle:** List units individually on Airbnb. Use solar/battery setups, composting toilets, and water delivery services if utilities are limited.
- **Example:** Three luxury tents at $150/night = $13,500/month gross at 100 percent occupancy

Upside: Fast to market
Bonus: Easy to remove or move units if zoning changes

Event-Driven Land Hack

- **How it works:** Build a photogenic structure (like a barn or dome) on a scenic property. Market it as a micro-wedding or retreat venue.
- **STR angle:** Rent to wedding parties, photographers, or corporate retreats and upsell lodging as part of the package
- **Example:** Mirror house + dome on five acres = $700/night + $2,000 wedding package on weekends

Upside: High-dollar weekends
Bonus: Repeat business through planners/vendors

Buy + Entitle + Flip or Partner Strategy

- **How it works:** Buy land that's underutilized or improperly zoned. Work with the city/county to get zoning changed or STR use approved.
- **STR angle:** Once entitled, flip to another STR investor or partner to build
- **Example:** Buy three acres for $90,000 → Entitle for five glamping units → Partner with builder or sell for $180,000+

Upside: Profit without building
Bonus: Creates off-market deal flow for your network

Creative Financing Strategies

Creative financing is often the key to getting your glamping business off the ground, especially if you don't have all the capital up front. Personally, I've used a mix of strategies—a HELOC on my primary residence, cash-out refinancing, and even 0% interest credit cards (which I don't recommend . . . but hey, I did it). I've also leaned on personal loans from platforms like SoFi, "buy now, pay later" options from glamping structure vendors, and, most importantly, strategic partnerships. For example, my partnership with ÖÖD Mirror Houses allowed me to access high-quality structures while keeping my capital focused on infrastructure as I built the site. Once you have a proof of concept like I did with first structure, it is much easier to present a feasible partnership model to potential partners.

There are several ways to reduce risk and stretch your budget: joint ventures with people who bring capital or construction expertise, revenue-sharing agreements with landowners in exchange for property access, and land leases—just make sure the lease terms are long enough to protect your investment. A phased development approach is also smart: Start with a few units, test the market, and scale with reinvested profits. Some people even mix these strategies—leasing land while using crowdfunding or partnerships to build the first units. My second glamping site is a mix of land leasing and partnerships where I leased land from a government park, partnered with ÖÖD Mirror Houses again, and have been able to expand my operations in a nearby market.

There's no one-size-fits-all formula, but the more resourceful and flexible you are, the more doors will open.

Building the Perfect Pitch

Most investors will be relatively new to trying to understand this niche of short-term rental investing. Now that there are several successful glamping sites around the globe, it will be easier to put together a presentation to potential investors. Highlighting the positives you can contribute and having a well-documented plan can help ease any investment worries and show that you are ready to take on the challenge.

My first partnership pitch didn't go nearly as well as I'd hoped. I had a connection with a major hotel developer and got the chance to present my glamping concept. I figured I could just lean on the hype: "People are crushing it with this all over the country, so why can't we?!" Spoiler: That pitch didn't land.

The potential partner hit me with a barrage of questions I wasn't remotely prepared to answer—things like projected annual revenue, estimated expenses, and even a full SWOT analysis. I mean, who would've guessed he'd want actual numbers before investing (insert heavy sarcasm here). Needless to say, I learned quickly that passion alone doesn't secure funding—preparation does.

Developing accurate and compelling financial projections is key to securing investor interest. Start with in-depth market research to determine revenue potential. Use tools like AirDNA, PriceLabs, and the BiggerPockets STR calculator (www.BiggerPockets.com/BookSTRCalc) to estimate nightly rates and analyze comparable properties, occupancy levels, and seasonal trends. Break down the financials into:

- **Projected revenue:** Show how revenue fluctuates by season, weekend vs. weekday rates, and premium add-ons like experiences or package deals
- **Operating costs:** Include maintenance, cleaning, marketing, insurance, and staff wages, if applicable
- **Profit margins:** Highlight anticipated net profits, break-even points, and return-on-investment (ROI) timelines
- **Sensitivity analysis:** Present best-case, worst-case, and base-case financial projections to demonstrate how the business can sustain fluctuations in demand

Investors want to see realistic and data-backed numbers that give confidence in the long-term profitability of your glamping site. Your pitch to investors needs to be polished, professional, and visually compelling to capture attention and build credibility. Explain the value you can bring to the table and how you will help solve a problem for the potential investor. A well-structured presentation should include:

- **Storytelling:** Highlight why the glamping market is growing, your site's unique features, and the demand for unique accommodations
- **Professional visuals:** Use renderings, drone footage, and high-quality images to showcase the design and layout
- **Market data and case studies:** Demonstrate comparable site success stories, traveler preferences, and glamping industry trends to reinforce demand

- **Financial breakdown:** Clearly outline cost estimates, expected revenue, profit margins, and investment returns using easy-to-follow charts and graphs
- **Exit strategy and growth potential:** Investors will want to know how they can profit from their investment over time. Discuss scalability, additional revenue streams, and long-term appreciation potential

Leverage industry data and insights from other glamping site owners to provide a realistic picture of costs for particular amenities or unique structures. Investors are more likely to commit when they can clearly visualize how their capital will generate strong returns.

Securing financing for a glamping project requires thorough preparation. Different lenders have different requirements, but the key aspects they assess include:

- **Business plan:** Banks and investors will expect a detailed road map outlining the glamping site's vision, market research, competitive advantages, operational structure, and revenue projections
- **Cash reserves and creditworthiness:** Lenders will want to see proof of liquidity and financial stability to ensure you can cover start-up costs and early operational expenses
- **Debt-service coverage ratio (DSCR):** Many lenders use DSCR to measure a project's ability to generate enough income to cover loan payments. A ratio above 1.25x is typically considered favorable
- **Zoning and permits:** Lenders will be more confident in financing a project if local zoning approvals and permits are in place or underway
- **Loan structure and collateral:** Understand the type of loan you are applying for—whether it's a traditional commercial loan, SBA loan, or private financing—and be prepared to offer collateral if required

By tailoring your pitch to match lender expectations and demonstrating that you have a clear grasp of the numbers, you position yourself as a credible borrower or investment partner. Overprepare for potential lender questions, and anticipate concerns they may have about the niche nature of glamping investments.

A well-structured investor presentation, backed by strong financials, market data, and lender preparedness, will significantly increase your chances of securing funding. Whether pitching to private investors, banks, or equity partners, your ability to demonstrate financial viability, risk management, and long-term scalability will set you apart in this growing industry.

Be prepared to negotiate terms such as repayment periods, interest rates, and payment schedules. Ensure the terms align with your business goals. These terms will vary greatly depending on what type of partnership you are developing. Before entering any agreement, please discuss with an attorney and understand your options when negotiating terms. There are two more common options: equity partnerships and debt financing.

Equity partnerships typically have a breakdown where one partner brings the capital and another partner brings the experience and sweat equity. Both investors can split up the capital requirements and sweat equity needed to get the venture off the ground. There is no exact method that needs to be followed. This will come down to what the specific deal entails and what both sides are aiming to accomplish with the project.

I have a friend who did a deal as a 50/50 equity split with their first partner, where the investor brought the $100,000 investment up front, and my friend brought around $25,000 plus the initial work to get the site underway. They split the cash flow 70 percent toward my friend for managing full time and 30 percent to the investor partner, with minimal work involved. When they decide to sell, they will be paid back their initial investment while equally splitting any profit in sales.

I have also seen deals done where one party puts no money down and the other investor party brought all of the capital. One brought the sweat equity, experience, and management skills to end up with a 20 percent equity split along with a 34 percent revenue share agreement. The investor took 80 percent equity and collected the rest of the revenue. They eventually sold for $2.3 million, after earning over $3 million in revenue in around five years. It was all what they felt comfortable with in the end, balanced with the value each side brought. Money does not have to be the only value a partner brings to the table.

One of my preferred, though more difficult, ways to work with an investor in your early stages is debt partnership financing, which allows investors to be the private lenders for your project. It will intrigue investors who believe in glamping and want to be as passive as possible. Terms can be negotiable here, but standard rates for private lending will be 2–4 percent higher than the current prime rate in the market. The repayment period is also negotiable and can range from two to twenty years, depending on what the lender has an appetite for. An initial investment fee may be referred to as "points," which equal 1 percent per point of the loan amount.

For example: If a private lender is lending $100,000 as an initial investment, they may negotiate an 11 percent interest rate, a ten-year repayment period, and two points (2 percent = $2,000).

Debt Partnerships vs. Equity Partnerships for Glamping

When financing a glamping project, choosing between debt partnerships and equity partnerships depends on factors like risk tolerance, control, and long-term profitability.

Debt Partnerships

Definition: One party provides capital as a loan, and the borrower repays it with interest.

☑ Pros:
- **Full ownership retention:** You maintain complete control over the business and future profits
- **Predictable costs:** Fixed loan payments make financial planning easier
- **Tax benefits:** Interest payments are tax-deductible
- **No long-term profit sharing:** Once the loan is repaid, the lender has no further claim on earnings

⊖ Cons:
- **Repayment obligation:** Loan payments must be made regardless of business performance
- **Credit and collateral requirements:** Lenders may require personal guarantees or property as collateral
- **Limited flexibility:** A portion of revenue must be allocated to debt service, reducing reinvestment opportunities

Equity Partnerships

Definition: Investors provide funding in exchange for ownership and a share of future profits.

☑ **Pros:**
- **No loan repayments:** Eliminates fixed debt payments, reducing financial strain in the early stages
- **Risk sharing:** Investors absorb some of the financial risks
- **More growth potential:** Additional capital allows for larger projects and expansion
- **Access to expertise and networks:** Equity partners often bring industry connections and strategic knowledge

⊖ **Cons:**
- **Loss of full ownership:** You give up a percentage of the business and its profits
- **Profit sharing:** Investors receive a portion of revenue indefinitely, reducing long-term earnings
- **Decision-making challenges:** More stakeholders can lead to conflicts over business direction
- **Exit strategy considerations:** Buying out equity partners or selling your stake can be complex

Choosing the Right Option for Glamping

Debt partnerships work best if you want to retain full ownership, have strong cash flow, and can handle loan payments. Equity partnerships are better suited for those seeking flexible funding, larger-scale development, or strategic partners. A hybrid approach combining both debt and equity may offer the best balance of risk and growth potential.

☑ PROS	⊖ CONS
Debt Partnership	
○ You keep full ownership after repayment	○ You owe the money no matter what
○ Clear repayment terms	○ More pressure to perform quickly
○ No profit sharing long-term	○ May require personal guarantees or collateral
○ Faster decision-making (no co-owners)	○ Limited flexibility if project changes

✅ PROS	⊖ CONS
Equity Partnership	
○ Share risk with partners ○ No fixed repayment schedule ○ Potentially easier to raise large amounts ○ Access to partners' networks, skills, and capital	○ You give up a portion of ownership ○ Profits must be shared ○ Decision-making can be slower or contentious ○ Exit strategies can get complicated

Showcase past successes, testimonials, or market trends that validate your vision. The more credible you appear, the easier it will be to secure funding and partnerships. If you have no experience, convincing anyone to take a chance on your idea will be more challenging. It's not impossible, but we must be realistic when approaching partners.

- How can you improve your credibility?
- Know your numbers inside and out from studying/consulting with glamping owners
- Acquire a property and have some invested into your venture already
- Work under local property management companies for short-term rentals
- Work under a local campground or glamping site to learn

Experience is always a key driver in building your credibility, but understanding your business plan and vision is the leading way to truly gather confidence from others.

Final Thoughts

One of the biggest challenges in glamping is the lack of traditional financing options. That's why cash reserves and creative strategies are often the most effective ways to get started. And here's the truth—the cash doesn't even have to be yours, and neither does the structure.

Understanding the business model and showing how to turn a site into a cash-flowing star is just as valuable as money in the bank. With the right pitch and the right partner, you might not need to invest a single dollar of your own.

But here's the golden rule: Any time you use someone else's money—whether it's a loan, partnership, or investment—treat it like it's worth twice as much as your own. Be smart and know your risk tolerance, and if glamping is your passion, don't be afraid to jump in and figure it out as you go.

Lessons from the Field

- **Get creative with capital.** I sold three condos for $40,000 profit, added $50,000 in savings, then filled the gap with a HELOC, 0% credit cards (not recommended, but real), and "buy now, pay later" programs from structure vendors.
- **Personal loans work.** Platforms like SoFi helped fund early builds when traditional financing didn't apply.
- **Partnerships can fuel growth.** I teamed up with ÖÖD Mirror Houses and used a land lease to expand without buying more property. Don't overlook joint ventures, seller financing, or revenue sharing with landowners.
- **Phased builds reduce risk.** I started with one dome, used the cash flow to fund more, and scaled intentionally.
- **Know your numbers.** My first pitch failed because I wasn't prepared. Investors want real revenue projections, costs, and ROI. Passion helps—but financials close the deal.

Part 2
Setting Up Your Glamping Site

Chapter 5

Site Development

Unless you're buying an already established campground, chances are you're about to become a land development wizard—whether you like it or not. This chapter covers everything from site layout and utilities to creating "wow factor" moments and smart ways to save money (and sanity) during the build-out process.

Development is easily one of the most expensive parts of launching a glamping site—but also one of the most important. I'll never forget the sticker shock of paying thousands just to lay gravel over a patch of grass. At this rate, I might need to start my own gravel company.

Land Assessment and Preparation

The foundation of any successful glamping site is choosing the right land and preparing it appropriately. A comprehensive land assessment ensures the property meets your business goals and supports the desired glamping infrastructure. You will be overwhelmed by the amount of available land options, but understanding what it takes to have the right piece of land for a successful glamping site will alleviate this issue.

Let me put this into an easier perspective. If guests won't instantly want to pull out their phone and start filming the property when arriving, then it probably is not the location you need. The power of word of mouth and social media on a glamping site's success rate is next level. Guests can be the ultimate ROI when they are paying to stay and also advertising for you at the same time.

Step 1: Analyze the Natural Features

Identify the unique characteristics of the land that can enhance the guest experience. Not all land is the same, and the more "wow factor" you have, the easier it will be to bring guests in. For example, does the property have:

- Scenic views, such as mountains, lakes, or forests?
- Natural features like streams, waterfalls, or wildlife?
- Accessibility to hiking trails, beaches, or national parks?

Highlighting these features can make your glamping site stand out and justify premium pricing. Preserve these natural elements as much as possible, as they are often the key selling point for eco-conscious travelers. These are not necessarily deal-breakers but will help you understand your target revenue potential when competing with sites with more premium features.

Step 2: Assess Topography and Soil Conditions

Topography plays a significant role in the layout and development of your glamping site. Steep slopes might offer stunning views but could increase construction and maintenance costs. Flat areas are easier to develop but may lack the appeal of elevated spots. Glamping is all about balancing these features while considering your budget and end goals.

Conduct soil tests to determine whether the land can support the infrastructure you plan to build. Can the soil handle septic systems or composting toilets? Is it stable enough for structures like domes, cabins, or elevated tents?

Hiring a professional surveyor to analyze the land will help you avoid costly surprises during development. You might be recommended to get a topography survey to show the change in elevation on the land at all points. Some counties may ask to see this to permit your building plans. These types of surveys are typically about two to four times as expensive as a regular survey and will increase depending on the land size and layout.

Step 3: Address Environmental and Legal Considerations

Before purchasing or developing land, check for potential environmental restrictions. This includes:

- Flood zones that may limit development or require additional insurance.
- Protected habitats for endangered species.
- Fire hazards in regions prone to wildfires.

Additionally, verify local zoning laws to ensure glamping is permitted. Contact the planning office to confirm that your intended use aligns with the property's zoning designation. If the land requires rezoning or a conditional use permit, factor the time and cost into your plans.

Step 4: Clear and Prepare the Land

Once the land is approved for development, it's time to clear and prepare it for infrastructure. You will need to remove brush, debris, and invasive plant species. Properly leveling your designated built sites will be required for whatever structure you plan. There must be designated walkways for each structure from your parking area. Keep inclines and the guest experience in mind when designing these walkways. Guests will need to bring luggage from your parking area and will not appreciate navigating through a pathway that doesn't exist up a steep incline.

Be mindful of preserving as much of the natural beauty as possible. Guests often choose glamping for its immersive outdoor experience, so excessive clearing can diminish the site's appeal.

Infrastructure Planning

A well-designed infrastructure is critical to your glamping site's functionality and guest satisfaction. Poor planning can lead to operational inefficiencies and negative reviews, so invest time in creating a comprehensive infrastructure plan.

Start by sketching a site map that includes:

- **Guest accommodations:** Where will tents, cabins, or domes be located? Consider spacing them far enough apart to ensure privacy while maintaining efficient land use.
- **Common areas:** Include spaces for communal activities, such as firepits, outdoor kitchens, or lounge areas
- **Parking and access roads:** Ensure vehicles can safely navigate the site without disturbing the natural surroundings

Work with an architect or landscape designer experienced in eco-tourism to create a layout that balances functionality with aesthetics. You will be able to use the land survey that you purchase to help them design an official layout. The topography survey mentioned earlier will also be handy here.

A major tip to save on costs up front for each unit is to plan your site around the current utilities or how they will be installed. If you build your first structure at the very back of your property, farthest away from utilities, you will be spending a premium. Instead, start with your first structure closest to the utilities already available or that will be installed.

If you have electricity at the front of the property, your first build should be as close as possible to that power pole, while also maintaining the guest experience and surroundings. The same goes for a water source, septic system, roadwork, and more. You then can keep building structures and progressing toward the farthest point of the land and keep utility installation as low an expense each phase as possible.

Developing glamping sites involves creating safe and accessible roads and parking areas. Poor access can deter guests and make logistics challenging for staff. The drive up is the first experience of the property, and if it is a massive struggle for the guest, you will be starting off on the completely wrong foot.

When developing your road system, it is smart to work with a local architect who can do site design to make sure all codes are accounted for. Some counties may require this depending on how many units you have to begin with. If you have one or two structures, the chances will be lower. Once you are planning more than three, be prepared to have a proper site design to show all of the parking and access ways based off the survey.

Access roads and pathways are essential for guests and service vehicles. One of the worst ways to cut off your revenue is having a poor road system requiring guests to own a four-wheel drive vehicle just to get to your glamping site. There are many options for what type of roadway you can build, which will vary depending on your budget. Your local area will have several road companies that you can get quotes from and see about reviews. You can reach out to local Facebook Groups to see if there is a local recommendation to make your choice even more confident.

The most expensive roadway will always be one made entirely of concrete, and unless you are reading this after winning the lottery, I would pass on this as an option. Use sustainable materials like gravel or crushed stone to minimize environmental impact while maintaining durability. These typically combine fair pricing with a long-lasting product. Over the first few years, you will learn where on your land water runs after rain and make a few adjustments with culverts and remedies.

Create clearly marked walking paths to guide guests to accommodations and communal spaces. Depending on the size of your operation, you will need to have ADA-compliant paths to accommodate guests with mobility challenges. Your site designer should be able to accommodate these needs and set up the proper layout according to compliance. After you have finalized your road system, regular maintenance of roads and pathways is essential to ensure safety and prevent erosion.

Strategic lighting is a crucial element in glamping site design, both for creating a welcoming atmosphere and ensuring guest safety. A well-lit environment allows guests to navigate the property comfortably at night while also serving as a deterrent to potential security risks.

When planning lighting, focus on key areas such as pathways, parking lots, access points, check-in areas, and communal spaces. These locations should have consistent, reliable illumination to prevent accidents and provide a seamless guest experience. Solar-powered or low-energy LED lights are excellent options, as they offer sustainability while reducing long-term electricity costs. Soft, warm lighting can enhance natural ambiance without feeling too harsh, ensuring guests still feel immersed in nature.

For service areas, storage spaces, and maintenance zones, motion-activated lights help minimize unnecessary energy consumption while reducing light pollution. These lights provide illumination when needed, improving security while keeping the natural night environment intact—an important factor for guests seeking a peaceful and remote escape.

Security is equally essential. Adding features such as gated entrances, coded keypads, and strategically placed security cameras can help monitor activity without being intrusive. Properly placed lighting around these areas ensures that guests and staff feel secure at all times. If the property is in a remote location, installing emergency call stations or panic buttons in key spots can further enhance safety and guest confidence.

The right lighting and security measures don't just protect guests—they enhance the overall experience by making the site feel well maintained, inviting, and professionally managed. Ensuring that guests can move around the property with ease at night will increase positive reviews and repeat visits, reinforcing the value of a well-thought-out lighting and security plan.

Utilities (Water, Electricity, Sewage)

Proper utility planning ensures a comfortable and enjoyable experience for guests. Depending on the location of your glamping site, you may need to get creative with off-grid or semi-off-grid solutions.

Reliable access to clean water is a top priority. Consider the following options:

- **Drilled wells:** Ideal for rural locations but require permits and professional installation. The number of units that can be powered by each well should be considered and discussed with a licensed water well company in your area.
- **Rainwater harvesting systems:** An eco-friendly option for areas with sufficient rainfall. Ensure water is filtered and treated for potable use. There may be additional permits needed from your local county if you are running a commercial facility, and this method will have the most hurdles.
- **Municipal water connections:** Convenient but may not be available in remote areas. If you have access to local water supplies, confirm with the local departments on costs and additional information you may need to plan for your glamping site.

Reliable water access is a critical factor in the success of a glamping site. Unlike traditional camping, where guests expect to "rough it," glamping provides a luxury experience that includes consistent water supply and pressure for showers, sinks, and other amenities.

To ensure an uninterrupted supply, water storage tanks should be installed as a backup system in case of well issues, municipal supply disruptions, or seasonal shortages. The size of the tank will depend on guest capacity, site location, and expected water usage. As a general rule, calculate daily water consumption per guest and ensure backup storage can last at least three to five days in case of an emergency.

Water pressure is just as important as availability. Without proper pressure regulation, guests may experience weak showers, slow sink drainage, or malfunctioning dishwashing stations. Installing pressure pumps or elevated water tanks helps maintain consistent flow, especially for sites with multiple structures or higher elevation changes.

For hot water, consider tankless water heaters to provide on-demand heating without the need for large storage tanks. These are energy efficient, take up less space, and ensure guests always have access to warm water. If your site is off-grid or reliant on well water, solar water-heating systems or propane-powered heaters can provide an eco-friendly alternative.

Glamping really ascended to its name when owners started offering refrigerators in units and places to charge your phone. Reliable electricity is mandatory at this point to truly provide a "glamorous camping" experience. What level of power you want provide is up to you, but consider the benefits of it. You need electricity for lighting, heating, cooling, refrigeration, amenities, and charging devices.

Luckily, you have a few different options in most areas.

- **Grid connections:** If available, this is the most straightforward option but may involve high installation costs in remote areas. Talk with local power companies to understand what typical costs are associated, and see if you can get some information to be more accurate on your numbers.
- **Solar power systems:** Eco-friendly and increasingly affordable. Include battery storage to ensure power availability during nighttime or cloudy days. These will not be able to power much, so consider your amenities that will include electricity. Make sure to do your research on the costs associated and the pitfalls of only having limited power.
- **Generators:** These are useful as a backup but are not ideal for long-term use due to noise and emissions.

I highly recommend trying to find properties that have power near the location so tapping into the local power supply is not an exorbitant amount up front. The more rural your property is, the more likely there is just one power supplier for the area, so getting a quote is typically pretty easy.

Handling waste responsibly is essential for maintaining environmental integrity. This will be one of your permitting department's top concerns and must be understood thoroughly before entering this venture. Options include:

- **Septic systems:** Common in rural areas but require proper soil conditions and regular maintenance
- **Composting toilets:** An eco-friendly alternative that reduces water usage. These work well for off-grid sites but require guest education
- **Municipal sewage connections:** Convenient but often unavailable in remote locations

When planning your site, it is crucial to figure out how many units you will eventually have so you can plan your septic systems from the beginning. Will you have one massive commercial unit or a few smaller systems connecting fewer units? If you plan with your septic, your costs will go down dramatically in the long run.

One of my glamping sites was initially planned for four more high-end units. An individual septic system would have cost around $10,000 per unit, but because I planned, my costs were about 50 percent of what they could have been. Yes, I had to put up $18,000 up front instead of just $10,000, but when I added another unit, I only had to pay for a lift station, which was $3,000. I added another two units and had to pay the same $3,000 per lift station.

For comparison:

1 unit per cabin: $40,000 ($10,000 for each unit built)
1 bigger system: $27,000 ($6,750 for each unit)

You will need to work with a registered sanitarian engineer in your county to design these systems, and most local septic companies will be able to help give quotes once the system is designed.

Plan for recycling and waste disposal areas to encourage guests to minimize their environmental impact. You will need to find out who the local trash collection company is and decide how much of a contract you need. Most units will require one garbage can to be dumped weekly, and once you have reached over four, a front dumpster with easy access for the trash company may be necessary.

Scenario	Total Cost	Units	Cost Per Unit
Individual Systems (One Per Unit)	$40,000	4	10,000
Larger Shared System	$27,000	4	$6,750

The Forgotten Details

Developing glamping sites involves creating safe and accessible roads and parking areas. Poor access can deter guests and make logistics challenging for staff. The drive up is the first experience of the property, and if it is a massive struggle for the guest, you will be starting off on the completely wrong foot.

When developing your road system, it is smart to work with a local architect who can do site design to make sure all codes are accounted for. Some counties may require this depending on how many units you have to begin with. If you have one or two structures, the chances will be lower. Once you are planning more than three, be prepared to have a proper site design to show all of the parking and access ways based off the survey.

Access roads should be wide enough to accommodate service vehicles, such as delivery trucks or emergency vehicles. They must be graded to prevent flooding and ensure safe navigation during inclement weather. Most importantly, you need durable, eco-friendly roads using compacted gravel or stabilized earth.

Include clear signage to guide guests to the site and their accommodations. Provide detailed driving instructions if the property is remote to ensure guests can find the location easily.

Parking areas should be conveniently located, without disrupting the natural surroundings. These areas should be should have clear signage options. Centralized parking lots near the entrance should have helpful carts that guests can pull to bring luggage to their unit and individual parking spots should be available near each unit that are designed to blend into the environment.

Making simple check-in videos showing how a guest drives up or arrives at their exact unit is beneficial to mitigate bad experiences at guest check-in. These messages can be automated in your property management system, and guests will appreciate a visual guide for arriving at a place they have never been before.

Ensure all access roads and parking areas are well lit and easy to navigate. Consider providing electric vehicle (EV) charging stations to cater to environmentally conscious travelers as well as providing options for guests who may arrive without vehicles, such as partnerships with local shuttle services or ride-share companies.

Sustainability is a core principle of glamping and should guide every aspect of site development. Guests often choose glamping for its harmony with nature, so maintaining environmental integrity is a moral and business imperative.

Reducing the ecological footprint of your development starts with thoughtful design. Focus on creating structures that naturally fit into the landscape, rather than forcing the land to fit your build. Elevating platforms for accommodations can also help minimize soil disruption, preserving the natural environment beneath. Additionally, it's important to avoid construction near sensitive ecosystems like wetlands or wildlife habitats to protect local biodiversity.

Using sustainable and locally sourced materials is another key strategy. Opt for options like bamboo or reclaimed wood for building cabins and decks, and consider installing solar panels and energy-efficient appliances for utilities. Even smaller choices, like offering biodegradable or recycled guest amenities such as toiletries and linens, can make a noticeable impact over time.

You can also invite guests to be part of your sustainability efforts. Provide clearly labeled recycling and composting bins throughout the property, and set up refillable water stations to help reduce single-use plastic waste. Including educational materials about your site's eco-friendly initiatives can help guests feel more connected to your mission and encourage them to adopt more sustainable practices during their stay.

Final Thoughts

The right piece of land can be the difference between a successful glamping site and a stressful one. Guests are willing to pay a premium for stunning views—but you'll pay a premium if you choose the wrong location. Utilities and infrastructure are some of the most expensive parts of development, so their feasibility should be a key factor in your decision.

When planning, put yourself in your guests' shoes. How will they experience the site from every angle—from the entrance to each cabin? That first impression, the moment they arrive and take it all in, sets the tone for their entire stay. Make it count.

Lessons from the Field

- **"Wow factor" drives bookings.** Unique designs and standout features make your site highly shareable, leading to organic marketing and higher occupancy.

- **Zoning laws can make or break your site.** Research local regulations early to avoid costly legal roadblocks that could halt your project.
- **Proximity to utilities saves money.** Building near existing power, water, and sewage lines reduces up-front infrastructure costs significantly.
- **Smart site planning pays off.** Thoughtful layout design lowers maintenance expenses and makes future expansion easier.
- **Water pressure matters.** Reliable plumbing and hot showers are nonnegotiable for guest satisfaction and repeat bookings.
- **Gravel roads prevent headaches.** Well-built access roads reduce wear and tear, keeping maintenance costs low and ensuring year-round accessibility.

Chapter 6

Accommodation Options

Before there were yurts and geo domes popping up on Instagram, French kings were escaping the city to build countryside retreats filled with gold ceilings, elaborate gardens, and fountains that ran twenty-four seven. It was the original luxury glamping—just with more powdered wigs and fewer composting toilets. In fact, King Louis XIV, in 1661, was one of the first to popularize this idea with the Palace of Versailles, a royal escape from Paris that became the blueprint for curated, short-term stays. While it wasn't exactly listed on Airbnb, the spirit of high-end, nature-connected hospitality started long before tiny homes and safari tents hit your feed.

When starting a glamping business, selecting the right accommodation type is one of the most critical decisions. Your choice will impact start-up costs, ease of permitting, guest experience, durability, and even the resale value of your property.

You should plan and consider what you want to do with the property in ten years. Are you planning to sell, expand, or hold long term? Your exit strategy or long-term ownership goals should influence your decision-making from day one.

This chapter explores various options, weighing their pros and cons to help you build a successful and profitable glamping site.

	✅ PROS	➖ CONS
Yurts	Spacious, easy setup	Needs maintenance, limited equity
Safari tents	Luxurious, affordable	Not weatherproof, short lifespan
Tree houses	High demand, unique	Expensive, tough permitting
Domes and pods	Weather resistant, trendy	Costly, insulation issues
Airstreams	Iconic, mobile	Small space, frequent upkeep
Shipping containers	Durable, eco-friendly	Costly mods, zoning issues
Conestoga wagons	Historic appeal	Limited space, insulation needed
Lotus Belle tents	Stylish, portable	Fabric wear, less insulated

	✅ PROS	⛔ CONS
Tiny homes	High resale, year-round use	Pricey, zoning challenges
Cabins	Strong equity, high demand	Expensive, large footprint

Each has trade-offs—choose based on budget, market, and long-term goals.

Types of Glamping Structures

Yurts. Timeless and spacious yurts have been used for centuries. Originating from Central Asia, they have become a popular modern glamping choice due to their spacious interiors, cozy insulated design, and visual appeal.

✅ **Pros:**
- Spacious and can accommodate larger groups
- Durable with the right materials
- Easier to transport and install
- Can be semi-permanent with a solid foundation

⛔ **Cons:**
- Requires ongoing maintenance, especially in humid or windy climates
- Does not add long-term real estate value
- Insulation and climate control need to be carefully planned

Safari tents. Safari tents provide a classic "tent with a twist" experience, immersing guests in nature without sacrificing comfort.

✅ **Pros:**
- High guest appeal, with strong marketing potential
- Can include full plumbing, AC, and heating
- Quick to install and relatively affordable

⛔ **Cons:**
- Not suitable for extreme weather conditions
- Canvas lifespan is limited, requiring replacement every five to seven years
- Lacks traditional property equity

Tree houses. Tree houses are among the most sought-after glamping stays, offering a nostalgic, childhood-inspired experience with high revenue potential.

☑ **Pros:**
- High occupancy rates due to uniqueness
- Social media appeal makes them easy to market
- Provides a bucket list experience that stands out on Airbnb
- More potential for property value appreciation compared to tents

⊖ **Cons:**
- Expensive to construct and maintain
- Requires extensive engineering and permitting
- Accessibility concerns for some guests

Pods and geodesic domes. Pods and domes have become popular due to their modern design, energy efficiency, and ability to create a unique guest experience. As someone who owns several geo domes, I can confirm they perform well, but they come with their own challenges.

☑ **Pros:**
- Strong weather resistance, if properly designed
- High demand among younger travelers and influencers
- Can be prefabricated for quick setup

⊖ **Cons:**
- Custom builds can be costly
- Climate control can be difficult without proper insulation
- Exterior canvas is challenging to keep clean and has a limited lifespan
- Some counties may not be familiar with permitting domes

Airstreams and vintage trailers. Airstreams and other vintage trailers bring a sense of adventure and nostalgia to glamping stays and have seen increased popularity in recent years.

☑ **Pros:**
- Strong brand appeal, with instant name recognition
- Movable and flexible for changing locations or reselling

- Easier permitting in some jurisdictions since they are not permanently affixed to the land

⊖ **Cons:**
- Limited interior space
- Require consistent and specialized maintenance
- Less investment upside compared to permanent structures

Shipping containers. Industrial and eco-friendly shipping containers have gained traction in the glamping industry due to their durability, modern appeal, and sustainable nature.

☑ **Pros:**
- Extremely durable and weather resistant
- Unique, modern aesthetic that appeals to design-conscious travelers
- Can be stacked or modified for larger accommodations
- Repurposing old containers promotes sustainability

⊖ **Cons:**
- Requires heavy insulation for temperature regulation
- Can be expensive to modify and transport
- Local zoning and permitting can be challenging

Conestoga wagons. Rustic and historic Conestoga wagons provide a pioneer-style glamping experience, offering an immersive and nostalgic stay for guests looking for a rustic, frontier feel.

☑ **Pros:**
- Distinct and highly marketable
- Compact yet comfortable interiors
- Appeals to families and history lovers

⊖ **Cons:**
- Limited space compared to other structures
- Weather protection may require additional insulation
- Less suitable for extreme climates

Lotus Belle Tents. Spacious and elegant, Lotus Belle tents offer a luxury twist on traditional camping, combining elegance with spacious interiors for an upscale glamping experience.

☑ **Pros:**
- Unique and Instagram-worthy design
- Quick to set up and remove
- More durable than traditional canvas tents

⊖ **Cons:**
- Fabric still requires periodic replacement
- Less insulated than permanent structures
- Susceptible to extreme weather conditions

Tiny homes. Small but functional, tiny homes are a popular alternative for glamping sites, offering all the comforts of a traditional home in a compact, energy-efficient space.

☑ **Pros:**
- Strong resale value compared to tents and domes
- Fully insulated and suitable for year-round use
- Market appeal to digital nomads and minimalist travelers

⊖ **Cons:**
- Higher up-front construction costs
- Requires appropriate zoning and permits
- Limited guest capacity per unit

Cabins. Timeless and reliable, cabins remain one of the most traditional and profitable glamping accommodations, offering guests a rustic retreat with modern comforts.

☑ **Pros:**
- Adds long-term real estate value to the property
- Suitable for year-round rentals with proper insulation
- High demand and strong occupancy rates

⊖ **Cons:**
- Higher build costs compared to temporary structures

- Requires larger land footprint
- Permitting can be more complex in certain areas

Each of these structures provides unique benefits and challenges, making it essential to choose the right fit based on market demand, budget, and operational goals. This is not an end-all list, and there are new glamping structures coming onto the market every day it seems. You will be surprised as to what you find draws your eye in with some dedicated searches online.

When I first got into glamping, I went all in on geodesic domes. I loved everything about them—the look, the buzz they created online, the lower build costs compared to other structures, and the fact that there were plenty of manufacturers to choose from.

But after living with them, I started learning what you don't see on Pinterest or in YouTube videos. Heating and cooling can be tricky. Keeping the exterior clean is more work than you'd expect. And there are a dozen small quirks you only discover once you actually own and operate one.

I say all this because even after nearly a year of research, I still missed some key things in my planning. What saved me? Talking to someone who had already built the exact structure I was considering. Asking the real, gritty questions.

Spending $100–$500 for solid advice from someone with firsthand experience is one of the best investments you can make. It'll save you way more than that in mistakes, missteps, and money down the road. Research who may have built the similar structures that you desire to build, and don't be afraid to book some consultation time with them. Spending this type of money up front can save you thousands of dollars going forward, and several headaches.

If you do purchase one of these types of products, please do not go the extra-cheap route. There is typically a reason one geodesic dome is $1,000 and another is $10,000. The quality in these types of structures can be a nightmare to maintain and a terrible experience for guests in a short time. Please buy high-quality products when dealing with major purchases or you will find yourself full of regret for trusting that random online website with "best deals."

Unique Builds—The Next Level of Glamping

Beyond traditional structures, some glamping operators are pushing boundaries with one-of-a-kind accommodations that not only attract more bookings but also create unforgettable guest experiences. These unique stays often lead to higher occupancy rates, premium pricing, and even media coverage, helping them stand out in a crowded short-term rental market. Airbnb even has its own category called "OMG" that explicitly pushes these type of accommodations.

Some of the most creative builds include:

- Converted grain silos.
- Glass or mirror cabins.
- Underground earth homes.
- Floating cabins for waterfront properties.
- Lighthouse-style stays.

The more unique the structure, the greater the potential for premium pricing and media exposure. These properties often gain traction on social media, travel blogs, and even TV features, providing free marketing and organic buzz that standard listings rarely achieve. However, custom builds come with challenges—they often require specialized construction, longer permitting processes, and increased up-front investment. Local zoning laws may not account for unconventional structures, meaning extra due diligence is necessary before breaking ground.

After exploring several structure types early on, I pivoted to mirror cabins—and it turned out to be one of the best decisions I made. These unique builds don't just turn heads—they do the marketing for you.

They create that instant scroll-stopping effect on social media, which drives awareness and bookings effortlessly. What's even better? The buzz they generate lifts the performance of your other less-unique units too. Occupancy across the board gets a boost.

The numbers speak for themselves—mirror cabins can often pay for themselves within just a couple of years. But before jumping in, make sure your market can support the nightly rates these units command. A high ADR means nothing if demand isn't there or if you're entering a market that's already saturated.

For investors willing to navigate these hurdles, the payoff can be huge. A well-designed, unique stay can command significantly higher nightly rates, maintain year-round demand, and create a viral brand identity—turning a single rental into a destination in itself.

Prefab Homes vs. Custom-Built Models

Prefab Homes—Fast and Scalable
Prefabricated tiny homes and cabins are an excellent option for those who want a durable, semi-permanent structure with minimal on-site labor.

☑ **Pros:**
- Faster installation
- Predictable costs
- Often come with preapproved plans for permitting

⊖ **Cons:**
- Limited customization
- It may not hold long-term equity like a traditional custom-build

Custom-Built Homes—The Long-Term Play
If you want to maximize equity and cash flow, a custom-built unit offers full creative control and better long-term value.

☑ **Pros:**
- Higher property valuation potential
- Full control over layout, materials, and guest experience
- Can be designed specifically for your market

⊖ **Cons:**
- Longer permitting and development process
- Requires more up-front capital
- Finding an architect who specializes in unique builds can be challenging

While prefab homes can be a fast and cost-effective way to set up a glamping site, custom-built structures offer greater long-term value, flexibility, and profitability. A thoughtfully designed, permanent build not only adds to the land's value but also allows for higher nightly rates, increased equity, and more control over the guest experience. Unlike prefabs, which may depreciate or limit resale potential, a custom structure can be fully integrated into the landscape, designed with premium materials, and built to last.

To maximize your investment, it's essential to work with an architect experienced in high-level, unique builds. The right architect will help ensure that your structure is not only aesthetic and functional but also efficiently designed for zoning, permitting, and long-term sustainability. Ideally, you'll find someone with a portfolio of creative projects, such as tree houses, domes, glass cabins, or eco-lodges, who understands the complexities of nontraditional hospitality builds.

An architect with experience in unique structures will:

- Optimize land use to take advantage of views, terrain, and natural features.
- Ensure compliance with local building codes and permitting requirements, avoiding costly delays.
- Incorporate eco-friendly design elements, such as passive heating, off-grid utilities, and sustainable materials.
- Create a design that enhances guest appeal and justifies premium pricing.
- Future-proof the build by making it adaptable for expansion, resale, or repurposing.

Beyond just hiring an architect, look for builders and contractors familiar with high-end custom stays. Prefab companies often follow cookie-cutter models, but a unique build requires craftsmanship that balances functionality, durability, and guest experience.

While the up-front investment for a custom-built glamping unit is higher than a prefab, the return is significantly greater. You gain a one-of-a-kind asset that stands out in a competitive market, maintains higher occupancy and nightly rates, and increases the overall value of your property—whether you keep it long term or eventually decide to sell.

With so many options, how do you decide what's right for your glamping site?

Consider:

- **Local demand.** What type of guests are booking in your area?
- **Climate.** Can your structure handle year-round weather?
- **Competition.** What are other successful glamping sites offering?

- **Permitting hurdles.** What does local zoning allow?
- **Scalability.** Can your structures allow for easy expansion?

A balanced glamping site might include:

- One to five permanent structures for higher-value bookings.
- One to five nonpermanent units for quick cash flow.
- One to five unique builds to create a standout brand.

You need to consider your overall design and the unity that will extend throughout your site. If you are going for luxury on some structures, you will need to keep that theme throughout the property. If you are going for more budget-friendly stays, don't expect to add a top dollar ADR unit in the middle and give the same guest experience they would expect.

Sourcing and Procurement—Getting the Best Deals

Sourcing structures for a glamping business requires a strategic approach to balance cost, quality, and efficiency. One of the best ways to maximize value is by buying directly from manufacturers, cutting out middlemen, and securing better pricing. Many manufacturers also offer customization options, ensuring the structures fit your specific design and operational needs. While it may be tempting to choose the cheapest option, cutting corners on quality can lead to higher maintenance costs, repairs, and replacements, ultimately costing more in the long run.

Considering used options—particularly for high-demand structures like Airstreams—can be a smart move for those looking to reduce up-front expenses. Well-maintained, pre-owned units often provide durability and aesthetic appeal at a lower price point. Another key strategy is partnering with builders who offer financing options, allowing for manageable payment structures rather than enormous up-front costs.

Additionally, leveraging bulk orders when purchasing multiple units can lead to significant discounts, making it easier to scale a glamping site efficiently while maintaining high-quality accommodations. Investing in well-built, durable structures ensures a more sustainable and profitable operation.

Each structure type has unique installation and upkeep needs.

- Safari tents and yurts require regular re-tensioning and weatherproofing
- Geo domes may need insulation upgrades for extreme climates
- Tree houses require periodic structural inspections for safety
- Airstreams demand RV-specific maintenance

The more complex the build, the more maintenance costs will affect your profits. These expenses should be factored into your financial projections.

Choosing the proper glamping structure is one of the most significant factors in long-term profitability. Whether you go with permanent structures, nonpermanent units, or a mix of both, your choices should align with your market, budget, and long-term vision for growth.

Final Thoughts

Choosing the right glamping structure—whether it's your first or your next—is one of the most important decisions you'll make. It's easy to fall into a rabbit hole of options, but don't lose sight of what truly matters.

Avoid going cheap. Skip anything that doesn't make you say "wow." Be clear on your end goals—are you optimizing for equity, cash flow, or both? And always factor in your market demand and local climate.

Lessons from the Field

- **Plan for the long-term.** Your structure choice should align with whether you plan to sell, expand, or hold the property.
- **Unique stays = higher rates.** Tree houses, domes, and mirrored cabins stand out but require specialized architects and longer permitting.
- **Permitting can be a hurdle.** Some counties don't know how to classify nontraditional builds, so check local regulations early.
- **Cheap builds cost more.** Low-cost structures lead to high maintenance and replacement costs—invest in quality materials.

- **Mix structures for balance.** Combine permanent builds for equity, nonpermanent for cash flow, and unique stays for social buzz.
- **Stay adaptable.** The glamping industry evolves fast—research, innovate, and build for long-term profitability.

Chapter 7

Amenities and Facilities

When I opened my first glamping site, I was so focused on getting the structures right that I didn't think through the full scope of operations. I figured I could stash a few supplies in a small carport on-site, and even left some storage items near the geo dome. My logic? Guests wouldn't care if things were out of sight.

Then I invited a fairly well-known influencer to stay and help build some early buzz. She arrived, looked around, and immediately started picking the place apart—specifically calling out the way storage was handled and saying she couldn't possibly showcase the space to her "precious" audience.

Now, she had her own vibe (not every content creator acts like they're god's gift to Instagram, so don't let one bad experience scare you), but her feedback was valid. I realized I had obsessed over the structures but hadn't fully thought through what it means to host. The guest experience includes everything—what they see, what they don't, and how it all feels.

Creating a well-thought-out glamping site requires more than just unique accommodations. Your amenities and facilities can significantly impact guest satisfaction, encourage positive reviews, and increase repeat bookings. While guests come for the experience of nature, they still expect a certain level of comfort, convenience, and thoughtful design.

Your market will help determine what will be successful and how you should approach these amenities and facilities. Studying other successful glamping sites or reflecting on your experiences when visiting glamping locations can provide valuable insights into how different setups function. Glamping sites need to be lean in operations but efficient in achieving a high level of hospitality. Let's explore the essential amenities and facilities contributing to a seamless and enjoyable glamping experience.

The Main Facilities

Most glamping sites do not have a reception area, which may be unnecessary. The larger your operation, the greater the chance you will need some type of reception, but with virtual assistants,

AI-automated messaging, and well-structured systems, you can keep this cost minimal while still providing a seamless experience. Many guests appreciate a self-check-in and self-checkout feature, making their arrival and departure smooth and efficient.

A well-designed common area enhances the social aspect of glamping and provides a space for relaxation, interaction, and convenience. Depending on the price point of your glamping site, these areas may include a pool, community hot tub, grilling stations, and other amenities that guests are comfortable sharing. Many of these amenities—especially hot tubs—should be private to match guest expectations if you are targeting higher-end guests and charging premium rates.

- **Check-in and welcome area**: Whether staffed or self-service, guests should have a smooth check-in process, with clear directions and an introduction to the property. Digital kiosks, key lockboxes, and easily digestible guidebooks or walk-through tours can streamline this experience and eliminate the need for a reception desk.
- **Outdoor lounge spaces**: Firepits, seating areas, hammocks, and shaded picnic tables create inviting communal spaces where guests can unwind and interact.
- **Wi-Fi and charging stations**: While many glamping sites promote a digital detox, providing optional Wi-Fi zones or charging stations in communal areas can enhance guest convenience. If guests pay a premium, they will likely expect Wi-Fi at their unit, so setting clear expectations up front is essential.
- **Informational boards or welcome books**: Maps, activity schedules, local recommendations, and emergency contact details should be easily accessible. Each unit should have a digital guidebook with a QR code that guests can scan to access all necessary information. This guidebook should be sent to guests at least a week before arrival and include Wi-Fi codes, activity suggestions, and emergency contacts.

High-quality restrooms and shower facilities are nonnegotiable for most glamping guests. This is one of the key factors that elevates glamping beyond traditional camping. The experience should be clean, comfortable, and well maintained. How you arrange your bathroom and shower facilities will depend on your budget, site layout, and the nightly rates you aim to achieve.

- **Private en suite bathrooms**: High-end glamping sites typically require private bathrooms that allow guests to stay in their units without needing shared facilities. Many premium glamping sites offer these bathrooms inside the unit or as private detached facilities.
- **Shared bathhouses**: If private bathrooms are not feasible, well-designed communal restrooms should include spacious, well-ventilated stalls, hot water showers with private changing areas, high-quality eco-friendly toiletries, proper lighting, and secure locks.

Hot water is a nonnegotiable for any glamping site. You should always have it available, with backup systems in place in case something fails. If guests go without it, be prepared to offer a refund—because they'll expect nothing less. Shared bathrooms and showers also need to be well lit and properly ventilated to ensure comfort. And no matter what type of bathroom setup you have, daily maintenance and cleanliness should always be a top priority.

Glamping guests often enjoy cooking their meals but expect a well-equipped space to do so. Whether you provide private kitchenettes, communal kitchens, or an on-site café, these areas should be designed for ease of use and efficiency.

- **Private kitchenettes**: Most glamping units should include a private kitchenette with amenities such as a mini-fridge, electric stovetop, cookware, microwave, air fryer, and other essentials that allow guests to prepare meals comfortably.
- **Communal kitchens**: If private kitchens are unavailable, shared kitchens should include gas or electric stoves, outdoor barbecue grills, firepits, utensils, dishwashing stations, and designated food storage areas. Each unit should have its own barbecue pit or grill at a minimum.
- **On-site restaurants or food service**: High-end glamping sites sometimes offer farm-to-table dining, breakfast bars, or food trucks. However, this requires significant operational expertise and typically only makes sense for larger sites with fifteen or more units.

Adding fun, well-chosen amenities can dramatically increase guest satisfaction, encourage repeat stays, and create buzz-worthy moments that fuel your marketing. While not every amenity needs to be expensive, a few key upgrades can make your glamping site stand out. Here are the top-ranked amenities based on impact, guest appeal, and ROI, along with estimated price ranges.

- **Hot tub:** $3,500–$8,000 The number one guest-requested luxury feature. Works in all seasons and creates strong visual appeal for listings. It requires more maintenance and a trained staff to take care of it, but the potential higher average daily rate and occupancy rates will make up for it.
- **Cowboy pool (stock tank pool):** $400–$1,200 Great for warm climates, low maintenance, and highly Instagrammable
- **Sauna (barrel or prefab):** $3,000–$6,500 Offers a unique wellness experience, adds winter appeal, and justifies premium nightly rates

Beyond the top-tier amenities, there are several midrange options that add charm and playfulness to the guest experience. These encourage guests to stay longer on the property and leave more detailed, glowing reviews.

- **Putting green:** $2,000–$5,000 Fun and unique, especially for golf lovers. Works well in open spaces with minimal landscaping.
- **Outdoor games (cornhole, giant Jenga, bocce, ladder toss):** $100–$300 Perfect for families or groups. Affordable and easy to rotate seasonally.
- **Board games (UNO, Scrabble, Catan, etc.):** $75–$200 Great for rainy days or cozy nights in. A thoughtful, low-cost way to round out the indoor experience.

Lastly, if you want to surprise and delight your guests, consider adding bonus features that tap into emotion, nostalgia, or personal connection. These touches aren't just fun—they become part of the story guests tell others.

- **Outdoor movie setup (projector and screen):** $250–$1,000 Creates a magical, memorable evening experience under the stars
- **Hammocks or hanging chairs:** $100–$300 Simple and serene. Ideal for couples or solo travelers.
- **Yoga mats and sunrise deck space:** $50–$150 Wellness focused and easy to incorporate into small outdoor areas
- **Guest journal or Polaroid station:** $50–$200 Adds a sentimental, shareable element to the stay—and creates future marketing material too

A successful glamping site should offer activities that encourage exploration, relaxation, and social engagement. Designing multipurpose spaces enhances the guest experience by providing on-site recreation and entertainment.

- **Outdoor lounges and firepits**: Ideal for socializing and relaxation
- **Game and entertainment areas**: Recreation huts with board games, cornhole, and a small library can add a fun element
- **Event spaces**: If hosting weddings, corporate retreats, or workshops, ensure your site has the infrastructure to support these gatherings, including road access, septic capacity, and insurance coverage
- **Nature trails and guided experiences**: Marked hiking and biking trails and scheduled outdoor activities can add value to a guest's stay

Behind every well-run glamping site is a strong operational backbone. Having designated storage and maintenance areas ensures smooth operations and high guest satisfaction. Don't end up with an influencer being the one to tell you how your storage game is in dire need of a revival.

- **Linen and supply storage**: Keep extra bedding, towels, and toiletries in a climate-controlled space
- **Outdoor equipment storage**: Essential for rental gear such as kayaks and bikes

- **Food and beverage storage**: Necessary if offering food service, ensuring proper refrigeration and pantry storage
- **Laundry facilities**: On-site washing machines and dryers help maintain linens for high-turnover properties
- **Waste management areas**: Implement a transparent trash disposal, composting, and recycling system
- **Water and septic systems**: Regular maintenance of water sources and plumbing is crucial for efficient operations

These buildings should be kept out of sight from guest areas to preserve aesthetics and follow a structured inventory system to prevent shortages. Regular inspections and team meetings can help identify maintenance needs and ensure smooth operations.

A successful glamping site is more than just a beautiful accommodation—it is a well-designed experience that balances nature and comfort. Investing in high-quality amenities and facilities creates a space where guests feel welcome and your operation runs smoothly. Prioritizing comfort, convenience, and thoughtful design will set your glamping business apart and create a memorable outdoor experience that keeps guests returning.

Final Thoughts

When I launched my first glamping site, I was laser focused on building a beautiful structure—but I overlooked the full guest experience. That oversight cost me an early opportunity and taught me a lesson I now pass on often: It's not just about the unit; it's about the entire operation. From proper storage to daily maintenance, every detail matters. A truly successful glamping site balances aesthetics, functionality, and hospitality. Design your space like a guest will see everything—because they will.

Lessons from the Field

- **Guests expect comfort.** Glamping is about nature *and* convenience, so invest in thoughtful amenities.
- **Self-check-in is key.** Automated check-ins with digital guidebooks and clear directions improve the experience.
- **Bathrooms matter.** Hot water, proper ventilation, and daily maintenance are nonnegotiable for guest satisfaction.

- **Kitchens should be well equipped.** Whether private or communal, clear instructions, stocked basics, and organization enhance the experience.
- **On-site activities boost value.** Firepits, wellness areas, and nature trails increase guest engagement and length of stay.
- **Strong operations = better reviews.** Organized storage, maintenance, and waste management keep the site running smoothly.
- **Plan for scalability.** Design multiuse spaces and infrastructure that allow for growth without major disruptions.

Part 3
Operations and Management

Chapter 8

Daily Operations

If we're going to talk about managing operations, we have to talk about the goat sacrifice story.

Let me preface this by saying that 97 percent of my guests are amazing. Thoughtful, respectful, sometimes even inspiring. I once even helped a guest get hired by a local company because they happened to be in the exact trade that company needed. So trust me—I've had plenty of "Airbnb restores my faith in humanity" moments.

But no number of great reviews or guest experience planning could've prepared me for this one.

I'll keep it brief. A guest booked our largest house for a week shortly after we launched it. I was still building on the back of the property at the time, so I'd drive by often. Everything seemed fine, though I did notice one odd thing: Everyone I saw outside (maybe three people max) was wearing some kind of white robe. Strange, but not alarming—yet.

The night before checkout, I got ten to fifteen motion alerts from our exterior cameras (if you don't have cameras, get them). It was 3 a.m., and I spotted someone walking around in what looked like a more official ceremonial robe. No idea what was going on.

The next morning, I arrived early to resume construction and ...yeah. In the field near the house, there were clear signs of a goat sacrifice. I won't go into detail, but it was one of those *Is this real life?* moments. I immediately called Airbnb and the local sheriff. Airbnb was surprisingly helpful—they approved a $3,000 payout for a hazardous-waste-removal crew to come out. The sheriff, unfortunately, said they couldn't do anything due to freedom of religion.

But the part that stuck with me most? When I called my Superhost support line and said, "Hi, I'm calling because there's been a goat sacrifice at my property," the rep paused and said, "Wow. I've been here seven years and never heard anything like this. I need to escalate this."

I share this not to scare anyone off, but to make a point: You cannot prepare for everything in this business. What you can do is build solid systems, strong boundaries, and a plan for when the unthinkable happens.

If you're planning to open a glamping site, you're not just setting up a few cool structures—you're launching a full-fledged hospitality business. And if you're not careful, it can quickly become a full-time job you never meant to sign up for. I still work a full-time job and manage two successful glamping sites, with more on the way.

How?

Because I built systems and operations that run the business without needing me in the day-to-day. I put in the work up front to create a *business*, not another job. That's the key: Don't get stuck working in your business. Focus on building it, so you can keep working on it—scaling, improving, and actually enjoying the freedom you set out to create in the first place.

Running a successful glamping business requires strong operational management, particularly in the areas of cleaning, maintenance, staffing, and emergency planning. The day-to-day operations will determine the overall success of the property, as cleanliness and efficiency directly impact guest experience and reviews. A well-organized approach to operations ensures that your rental remains competitive, highly rated, and profitable.

Cleaning Operations

For smaller operations of eight units or fewer, you can typically get away with managing the cleaning process through a team of at least two professional cleaners, though having three or four is ideal. A minimum of two cleaners is necessary in case one is unavailable due to illness or other emergencies. As the number of properties grows, consider adding one cleaner for every two additional units. If you manage multiple properties, you might find it beneficial to create a structured schedule for your cleaning team to ensure seamless transitions between bookings. Keeping your cleaning team efficient and motivated requires clear expectations, standardized procedures, and appropriate compensation that aligns with the local market.

Before hiring cleaners, it is best to test their skills by having them clean a unit before any guests arrive. This allows you to evaluate their thoroughness and attention to detail. When hiring new cleaners, ensure they understand the unique demands of STR cleaning compared to traditional residential cleaning. Cleaners can be sourced through local Facebook Groups, Turno, Tidy, and other job platforms that specialize in hospitality services. It is important to collect a W-9 from each cleaner to ensure compliance with tax reporting. If a cleaner earns more than $600 in a year, you are required to send them a 1099 form, and your bookkeeper or CPA can help with this process. While most STR owners rely on 1099 contractors, some opt to hire W-2 hourly employees for greater control and consistency. If you scale to a level where full-time cleaning staff makes sense, consult with your accountant and attorney to ensure that the hiring process complies with local labor laws. Understanding the difference between hiring contractors and employees will help you avoid legal issues and ensure smoother operations in the long term.

Cleaners should always be trained to follow a standardized cleaning process, which includes taking detailed photos before and after each clean. This helps protect against guest complaints and ensures proper documentation of the property's condition. One of the most common guest complaints involves claims of dirty bedding. To mitigate this, cleaners should photograph each stage of bed-making, including fitted sheets, flat sheets, and comforters. Additionally, they should report any damages or missing items promptly so that claims can be filed in a timely manner. STR hosts must also consider the frequency of deep cleaning to maintain high cleanliness standards. In addition to routine turnovers, properties should undergo deep cleans at least quarterly or biannually. This involves addressing often-overlooked areas such as baseboards, air vents, windowsills, and under furniture. The goal is to maintain the highest level of cleanliness to prevent negative guest feedback and maintain longevity in the market.

Cleaning rates will vary by location, so it is beneficial to call at least three local cleaning companies to gather pricing data. Many cleaning processes can also be automated by syncing property management systems with cleaning platforms like Turno or Breezeway. These tools help streamline scheduling, tracking, and communication with cleaners, making it easier to manage multiple properties at once.

Handling Maintenance

Beyond cleaning, maintenance is another critical aspect of daily operations. Keeping a well-maintained property requires having a list of reliable subcontractors for electrical work, plumbing, septic issues, HVAC, appliances, and roadwork. These professionals should be vetted carefully by checking their licenses, ensuring they carry liability insurance, and testing their work on small projects before hiring them for larger jobs. It is helpful to compile a list of subcontractors by searching Google, checking Facebook Groups, and asking real estate agents for recommendations. All subcontractors should provide a W-9, and payments should be documented for tax purposes. By having a solid list of go-to subcontractors, you ensure that issues are resolved quickly without compromising guest experience.

In addition to subcontractors, having a reliable handyman on call is essential for handling minor repairs such as loose door handles, drywall fixes, tile cracks, and fence repairs. Finding a handyman within a thirty-minute radius of your property is ideal, as this allows for quick response times to urgent repairs. Like subcontractors, handymen should have liability insurance, provide references, and be given small test projects before taking on larger tasks.

Staffing a Glamping Business

Staffing beyond cleaning and maintenance depends largely on the scale of your STR operation. For smaller setups, there is typically no need for a dedicated check-in clerk, as most check-in processes can be automated. Property management systems like Hospitable can sync with smart locks to provide guests with unique entry codes, eliminating the need for manual key exchanges. Apps that verify guest IDs and provide damage protection can further streamline operations. It is also advisable to set up a business phone line through services like OpenPhone or Google Number, which allows team members to access messages and calls from their own devices without requiring a separate phone.

Handling guest inquiries and support can often be managed independently for smaller properties, as guest calls are typically infrequent. However, as the number of units increases, hiring a virtual assistant (VA) can significantly improve guest communication efficiency. Initially, one VA can manage guest interactions for up to five properties, but as the business scales, additional VAs can be added. For every five to ten properties, adding another VA ensures that guest inquiries are handled promptly. For glamping sites with ten to twenty units, two VAs and a general manager overseeing operations is usually sufficient. VAs can be sourced from platforms like Upwork, where experienced candidates with Airbnb-specific knowledge can be found.

Key Members Order of Hiring Chart & How to Find Them	
Cleaners	Local Facebook Groups, Turno, Google
Handyperson	Local Facebook Groups, Thumbtack, Angi, Google
Subcontractors	Local Facebook Groups, Thumbtack, Angi, Google
Social media managers	Fiverr, Upwork, Instagram
Operations team (inpsector, guest services, on-site)	Local Facebook Groups, friends and family, local references
Marketing manager	Indeed, Upwork, ZipRecruiter

As your glamping business scales, building the right team becomes crucial for efficiency, guest satisfaction, and brand growth. While cleaning and maintenance are essential, additional team members can help optimize operations, enhance guest experiences, and increase visibility.

- **Social media manager:** A strong social media presence can drive direct bookings, create brand loyalty, and increase engagement. A dedicated social media manager can handle content creation, influencer partnerships, and targeted advertising, ensuring your glamping site stays top of mind for potential guests.
- **Pre-check-in unit inspector:** This role ensures cleanliness and quality control before guests arrive. By inspecting units, taking photos, and verifying everything is guest ready, an inspector prevents complaints and negative reviews related to cleanliness or missing amenities
- **Marketing manager:** Unlike a social media manager, a marketing manager focuses on the bigger picture—running ad campaigns, managing your website's SEO, and creating strategies to increase occupancy and direct bookings. They may also oversee email campaigns and referral programs to keep past guests engaged.
- **Public relations (PR) manager:** If you want media coverage, influencer collaborations, and press opportunities, a PR manager can be a game changer. They can secure magazine features, travel blog write-ups, and media placements to increase your brand's reach and credibility.

- **On-site maintenance and guest experience manager:** As operations grow, having an on-site manager can streamline maintenance, handle guest requests, and quickly resolve any issues. This role is particularly valuable for larger sites where response time is crucial.

Each of these roles adds value and enhances guest satisfaction, but hiring decisions should align with your business scale and revenue goals. Many of these positions can be outsourced or started as part-time roles, with expansion as your glamping site grows.

Procedures You Must Have

Standard operating procedures (SOPs) are critical for ensuring consistency in operations. SOPs should cover emergency situations, guest disturbances, septic system failures, water well issues, check-in procedures, weekly inspections, and any other potential challenges. Having clear SOPs in place allows for quick and efficient responses to unforeseen issues. Emergency situations in particular require well-defined protocols. For example, if a guest reports a fight or a disturbance, there should be clear guidelines on whom to contact and what steps to take. Security measures should also be in place, such as having surveillance cameras at property entrances to monitor comings and goings. It is advisable to install solar-powered cameras with LTE or Wi-Fi capabilities to maintain security and have a record in case of trespassing or other incidents.

The operational efficiency of a glamping business relies heavily on the systems put in place. By integrating automated processes for guest communication, cleaning, and maintenance scheduling, hosts can reduce the manual workload while improving consistency. Regularly reviewing operational procedures and adapting to new challenges ensures that the business remains resilient and profitable. The glamping industry continues to evolve, and staying ahead of operational challenges will position hosts for long-term success. Furthermore, investing in training programs for your staff and creating contingency plans for unexpected events will create a strong foundation that can withstand market fluctuations and guest expectations. The key to a successful glamping operation is consistency, attention to detail, and adaptability, ensuring that every guest enjoys a seamless, high-quality experience.

Final Thoughts

Running a glamping site isn't just about building unique spaces—it's about building a business that works even when you're not there. The day-to-day operations are where your guest experience is truly defined and where your brand earns its reputation. From cleaning to maintenance to staffing, every detail matters.

I've been able to scale while working a full-time job not because I hustle harder but because I put in the time early to create systems that keep things running without constant oversight. That's the difference between owning a job and owning a business.

If you want to grow, you need structure. SOPs, automation, a reliable team, and a clear vision of how your operation runs at scale are all essential. Whether you're managing one unit or twenty, your success will come down to how well your systems perform when you're not watching. Just be ready to spring into action if you see any goats coming in on your cameras.

Lessons from the Field

- **Cleanliness drives reviews.** Train cleaners, document with photos, and schedule deep cleans.
- **Fast maintenance prevents problems.** Keep a go-to handyman and vetted subcontractors on call.
- **Automation saves time.** Use smart locks, AI messaging, and property management systems.
- **VAs improve efficiency.** One VA can manage guest communication for up to five properties.
- **SOPs ensure consistency.** Have clear procedures for emergencies, check-ins, and maintenance.
- **Security is essential.** Use cameras, guest ID verification, and clear safety protocols.
- **Smooth operations = repeat guests.** Consistency and efficiency keep occupancy and ratings high.

Chapter 9

Guest Experience Management

Guest-experience management is one of the most critical components of a successful short-term rental business. A guest's first and last impression significantly influences their overall satisfaction, likelihood to leave a positive review, and potential to return for future stays. Effective management of the guest journey—from pre-arrival communication to post-checkout follow-ups—ensures a seamless experience that sets your rental apart.

I'll never forget the first time my digital keypad failed (better than anything to do with goats, though)—and I didn't have a backup lockbox nearby for the guest. I panicked. Luckily, my cleaner was still on-site with a spare key, but it could have easily turned into a disaster. It was a tough reminder that even small oversights can have a big impact on the guest experience.

Moments like that taught me the importance of thinking through every part of a guest's stay. From check-in to checkout, the details matter. Learn from my early mistakes—this chapter will walk you through how to prepare like a pro, so your guests feel taken care of from the moment they arrive.

Creating a Seamless Check-In and Checkout Experience

The check-in and checkout process sets the tone for a guest's stay. Ensuring these processes are as smooth and stress free as possible can prevent negative experiences before they arise.

Your check-in and checkout times should be clearly stated across all booking platforms, on your property's website, and in pre-arrival communication. Guests should never have to search for basic details like when they can arrive or when they need to depart. If early check-ins or late checkouts are available for an additional fee, make sure to clearly state this option up front.

Using smart locks with digital codes eliminates the need for physical key exchanges and provides flexibility for guests arriving at various times. Smart locks should be programmed with unique, temporary codes for each guest to enhance security and minimize issues related to lost keys. However, it is crucial to have backup solutions in place, such as a physical key stored in a lockbox. A hidden, secondary lockbox can serve as an additional emergency backup in case of malfunctions.

To reduce confusion and set clear expectations, consider sending a comprehensive check-in guide that includes:

- Step-by-step written instructions with photos for accessing the property.
- A YouTube video walk-through covering smart locks, Wi-Fi access, thermostat control, appliance use, and emergency procedures.
- Parking instructions, especially for properties with limited or street parking.
- House rules, emphasizing quiet hours, smoking policies, and pet restrictions, if applicable.
- Local recommendations, including restaurants, grocery stores, gas stations, and emergency contacts.

A well-prepared digital welcome book should be provided in both physical and digital formats, ensuring guests have easy access to all essential information throughout their stay.

Proactive Guest Communication

Sending an automated message around 7–8 p.m. on check-in day is a best practice to confirm that guests have settled in without any issues. This simple gesture allows you to address any minor problems early on, preventing them from escalating into major complaints.

Example message:

> *Hi [Guest Name], I hope you've arrived safely and are settling in comfortably! Please let me know if there's anything I can do to make your stay more enjoyable. Enjoy your time, and don't hesitate to reach out if you have any questions! —[Your Name]*

While communication is vital, excessive messaging can overwhelm guests. Structuring your communication with strategic touchpoints ensures guests receive the right information at the right time. Here's an effective timeline.

- **Instant booking confirmation email.** Confirms the reservation and provides an overview of what to expect.
- **Fourteen days before check-in.** A follow-up email with check-in details, local recommendations, and optional upsell opportunities (e.g., airport pickup, special packages).
- **Seven days before check-in.** A reminder about available add-ons like birthday/romantic packages or private chef experiences.
- **One day before check-in.** The most important communication: sending the entry code, detailed check-in instructions, and emergency contact information.
- **Post-check-in message (evening of arrival).** Checking in to ensure the guest has arrived without issues.
- **Mid-stay check (for stays of three-plus days).** A message to ensure everything is going well and to remind them of any ongoing services (e.g., housekeeping for longer bookings).
- **Checkout instructions (morning of departure).** A simple thank-you message with reminders for checkout procedures.
- **Review request (one day after checkout).** A request for a five-star review and an opportunity to provide private feedback.
- **Return guest incentive (two to four weeks post-stay).** A personalized discount code for future stays as a retention strategy.

Offering concierge services can elevate your short-term rental and help it stand out in a crowded market. You don't need a full-time concierge to make this work—a well-trained virtual assistant (VA) can handle most of it remotely. Personalized guest support, from answering questions to providing curated local recommendations, adds a thoughtful touch that guests remember and often mention in reviews. A solid concierge experience can turn a good stay into a great one.

Services like curated guides to the best restaurants, hidden gems, and local attractions help guests make the most of their trip. You can also assist with booking transportation such as rental cars, rideshares, or airport transfers. Stocking groceries and preparing and special occasion packages—like birthday, anniversary, or romantic setups—can surprise and delight guests. If your property is in a nature-driven location, offering adventure gear like bikes or kayaks can further enhance the experience. These extras not only boost satisfaction but can also lead to increased revenue and repeat bookings.

Guests are often willing to pay extra for convenience and unique experiences. Implementing upsell opportunities can increase revenue by 5–15 percent while making the stay more memorable.

Examples of Profitable Add-On Packages

- **Birthday Celebration Package ($75–$150)**
  - Cake or cupcakes
  - Balloons and banners
  - Personalized birthday card
  - Candles
  - A small snack package
- **Romantic Getaway Package ($100–$200)**
  - Rose petals and candles
  - Chocolate-covered strawberries or gourmet dessert
  - One or two dozen roses
  - Small snack package
- **Adventure Package**
  - Local activity guide with exclusive discounts
  - Packed picnic basket
  - Gear rental (e.g., hiking poles, bicycles, fishing equipment)
- **Private Chef or Catering Experience ($150–$500)**
  - On-site, chef-prepared dinner
  - Premade meal delivery service

Each package should be priced to ensure a minimum 50 percent profit margin after expenses. This additional revenue stream not only increases profitability but also improves guest satisfaction and review ratings. Deciding how to fulfill these packages varies in complexity depending on who handles them. If you are available to handle these and take all of the profit, then it's smooth sailing. Most people will need a third party to help fulfill these packages.

Maintaining high guest satisfaction requires a well-trained team and streamlined operations. Key elements of effective team management include:

- Training VAs to handle guest communication efficiently.
- Standardizing housekeeping procedures to ensure a consistent experience.
- Conducting routine property inspections to address maintenance before guests notice issues.
- Using property management systems (PMS) to automate check-in messages, reviews, and maintenance requests.

Final Thoughts

A well-executed guest experience strategy transforms a simple rental into a highly rated, profitable business. By implementing automated yet personal communication, streamlining check-in/checkout, offering upsell opportunities, and ensuring operational excellence, you can create an unforgettable stay that keeps guests returning and recommending your property to others. Prioritizing guest satisfaction doesn't just lead to higher reviews—it also results in higher occupancy rates, increased revenue, and a stronger long-term brand presence in the short-term rental industry.

Lessons from the Field

- **First impressions matter.** Smooth check-in/out boosts satisfaction.
- **Clear communication prevents issues.** Automated messages keep guests informed.
- **Smart locks save time.** Self-check-in with backups reduces confusion.
- **Strategic messaging works.** Guests get the right info at the right time.
- **Concierge services add value.** Upsells enhance stays and increase revenue.
- **Training ensures consistency.** Well-trained staff maintain high standards.
- **Great experiences drive growth.** Happy guests means better ratings and more bookings.

Chapter 10

Property Maintenance for Glamping Sites

"Your outdoor chair is broken" a guest messaged me one day. I apologized immediately and asked what had happened. His response? "I don't know, but when I sat in it, it instantly broke." Thankfully, I was able to smooth things over and still ended up with a five-star review (more on how I handled that in Chapter 13).

But that moment was a wake-up call. It made me realize how important it is to stay ahead of anything that could impact the guest experience. Preventive maintenance isn't optional—it's essential if you want to avoid surprises, protect your reputation, and keep those five-star reviews rolling in.

Maintaining a glamping property requires a proactive approach to ensure that structures, utilities, and amenities remain in top condition. Unlike traditional short-term rentals, glamping accommodations are exposed to the elements, making preventive maintenance, seasonal preparations, equipment upkeep, grounds maintenance, and waste management critical. A well-maintained site ensures guest satisfaction, extends the lifespan of expensive structures, and keeps operating costs in check.

Preventive Maintenance Schedules

Preventive maintenance is the backbone of any well-run glamping site. Because many glamping structures—such as safari tents, yurts, domes, and cabins—are built with alternative materials and exposed to weather fluctuations, they require specialized upkeep. Establishing a routine maintenance calendar helps prevent costly repairs and ensures that the property remains safe and functional for guests.

Daily and weekly maintenance tasks should focus on the essentials. This includes checking all anchor points for tents and domes, inspecting plumbing for leaks, ensuring that heating and cooling systems are functioning properly, and monitoring water levels in tanks if the site relies on rainwater collection or well systems. Outdoor elements such as firepits, seating areas, and decks should be inspected for safety, as exposure to moisture and UV rays can lead to deterioration over time.

More in-depth maintenance should occur on a monthly and quarterly basis. This includes deep cleaning all structures, flushing water heaters, lubricating hinges and locks, and trimming back vegetation that could pose a fire hazard or attract pests. Additionally, smoke and carbon monoxide detectors should be tested regularly to comply with safety standards. Annual maintenance should involve roof inspections, applying fresh weatherproofing treatments to wooden structures, and evaluating the overall condition of furniture, linens, and appliances.

Because glamping sites are often located in nature and rely on outdoor elements, seasonal changes can significantly impact operations. Preparing for shifting weather conditions is essential for preventing damage and maintaining guest comfort.

Spring is the time to inspect for any winter damage, such as leaks, fallen branches, or weakened structures. A thorough deep clean is necessary to remove any debris, mold, or mildew that may have accumulated. Outdoor amenities like pools, outdoor showers, and communal spaces should be prepared for increased use. If the site has gravel roads or pathways, adding fresh gravel can prevent mud buildup and improve accessibility.

As summer approaches, pest control becomes a major priority. Mosquitoes, wasps, and other insects can become a nuisance, so regular treatments and the addition of citronella torches or bug-repellent plants can help mitigate the problem. Cooling solutions such as shade structures, misting systems, or additional ventilation should be checked and reinforced to keep guests comfortable. Fire safety is also crucial in dry, hot climates, requiring regular inspections of firepits, extinguishers, and emergency protocols.

Fall is a transitional season that requires winterization preparations in colder climates. Plumbing should be insulated, outdoor water sources turned off, and emergency supplies like firewood and heating fuel stocked. Generators and backup power systems should be tested to ensure they are functioning properly. Fall is also an ideal time to conduct a final pest-control treatment before insects and rodents seek warmth inside structures.

In winter, freezing temperatures can cause significant damage if not properly addressed. Water lines should be drained, insulation should be checked for efficiency, and pathways must be kept clear of snow and ice to prevent guest injuries. If the site remains operational, heaters, fireplaces, and hot tubs should be regularly maintained to ensure they function safely.

Spring Maintenance

- Inspect for winter damage (leaks, fallen branches, weakened structures)
- Perform a deep clean of all units to remove debris, mold, and mildew
- Check and prep outdoor amenities (pools, showers, communal spaces)
- Add fresh gravel to roads and pathways for better accessibility

Summer Maintenance

- Implement pest control (treat for mosquitoes, wasps, and insects)
- Set up bug-repellent plants or citronella torches around guest areas
- Ensure cooling solutions (shade structures, misting systems, ventilation) are working
- Inspect fire safety measures (firepits, extinguishers, emergency plans)

Fall Maintenance

- Winterize plumbing (insulate pipes, shut off outdoor water sources)
- Stock firewood, heating fuel, and emergency supplies for colder months
- Test generators and backup power systems for reliability
- Conduct a final pest-control treatment to prevent winter infestations

Winter Maintenance

- Drain water lines to prevent freezing and bursting
- Check and reinforce insulation in units for energy efficiency
- Keep pathways clear of snow and ice to prevent guest injuries
- Maintain heaters, fireplaces, and hot tubs to ensure safe operation

Equipment and Structure Upkeep

Glamping structures require a level of care beyond traditional short-term rentals. Materials such as canvas, wood, and metal require specialized maintenance to prevent weather-related deterioration. Tents and domes, for example, must be regularly inspected for small tears or UV damage, and waterproofing treatments should be reapplied annually. Proper ventilation is essential to prevent condensation buildup, which can lead to mold or fabric degradation.

For cabins and tiny homes, checking for drafts and resealing doors and windows ensures that heating and cooling systems operate efficiently. Wood structures need periodic staining or sealing to prevent rot and insect damage. Additionally, checking for foundation shifts, particularly in areas prone to heavy rain or flooding, helps prevent long-term structural issues.

Tree houses and elevated structures require extra attention to stability. Support beams, fasteners, and suspension cables should be inspected regularly for signs of wear, as exposure to the elements can weaken them over time. Railings, ladders, and staircases must also be checked frequently to ensure guest safety.

Outdoor amenities such as hot tubs, saunas, and communal spaces also require regular maintenance. Hot tubs should be drained and cleaned frequently, with water chemistry tested to prevent bacterial growth. Wooden furniture and decking should be treated with weather-resistant coatings, while hammocks, swings, and outdoor seating should be checked for frayed fabric or loose bolts.

A well-maintained landscape enhances the overall glamping experience. Unlike urban short-term rentals, where curb appeal is defined by driveways and flower beds, glamping sites rely on their natural surroundings to create an immersive outdoor experience.

Regular lawn care, trimming overgrown vegetation, and clearing pathways ensure that guests can move around the property safely. In areas with heavy foliage, fallen leaves and branches should be cleared to prevent fire hazards and reduce pest infestations. If the site features gardens, these should be maintained seasonally, with appropriate irrigation systems in place.

For sites located near water bodies such as lakes, rivers, or ponds, erosion control is an important consideration. Installing gravel, stone barriers, or retaining walls can prevent soil loss and maintain the integrity of walking paths. Additionally, maintaining access points to natural water sources, such as docks or swimming areas, ensures they remain safe and functional.

Glamping businesses must also balance comfort with sustainability. Many guests are drawn to glamping because of its eco-friendly appeal, making responsible waste management a key operational component.

Proper waste disposal begins with providing clearly labeled trash and recycling bins throughout the site. Encouraging guests to sort their waste properly can be achieved through signage and educational materials. Composting is another great option for sites that offer farm-to-table dining or operate off-grid, helping to minimize food waste while enriching the soil.

For sites that rely on septic systems, regular maintenance is essential to prevent backups and leaks. Septic tanks should be inspected and pumped as needed, and guests should be provided with clear guidelines on what can and cannot be flushed. Sites using composting toilets must regularly manage waste disposal and ensure that ventilation systems are functioning properly.

Sustainable energy solutions, such as solar panels or wind turbines, require routine checks to ensure they are operating efficiently. Battery storage systems should be monitored to confirm that they are holding a charge, while backup generators should be tested periodically. These come with their own challenges and costs, so make sure to research before diving in headfirst.

Water conservation is another important aspect of sustainable glamping maintenance. Rainwater collection systems should be cleaned regularly to prevent contamination, and low-flow fixtures can help reduce water usage. Providing guests with reusable water bottles and refill stations further encourages sustainability while reducing the environmental impact of single-use plastics.

Final Thoughts

A well-maintained glamping property isn't just about appearances—it's the foundation of a successful, long-lasting business. Proactive maintenance reduces operating costs, protects your investment, and creates a consistently high-quality experience that keeps guests coming back.

By implementing a thoughtful plan that covers preventive care, seasonal prep, structural upkeep, landscaping, and eco-friendly waste management, you can operate efficiently while preserving the natural charm that draws people to glamping in the first place. When you invest in quality systems and materials up front—and maintain them with intention—you're not just maintaining a site; you're building a brand that can thrive for years to come.

Lessons from the Field

- **Preventive maintenance saves money.** Regular inspections prevent costly repairs.
- **Seasons affect operations.** Plan for weather, pests, and winterization.
- **Glamping structures need care.** Waterproof, ventilate, and inspect annually.
- **Outdoor spaces require upkeep.** Maintain hot tubs, firepits, and trails.
- **Landscaping improves experience.** Keep paths clear and manage erosion.

- **Sustainability matters.** Reduce waste and conserve water for efficiency.
- **Proactive maintenance protects profits.** A well-kept site keeps guests happy and costs low.

Part 4
Marketing and Sales

Chapter 11

Marketing Strategy

Luckily, I was able to bounce back from an influencer telling me my place wasn't "fit" for their page. Today, we've built a recognizable brand with over 60,000 social media followers, 5,000 engaged newsletter readers, a 3:1 return on every dollar spent in paid ads, and viral videos reaching over a million views. None of that happened by chance—and it certainly wasn't free. Getting to this level required a marketing mindset *and* a real budget. If you want to scale, you have to treat marketing like an investment, not an afterthought.

Successfully marketing a glamping business takes more than just posting pretty pictures. It requires a full-stack approach—clear brand identity, a strong digital presence, engaging content, strategic partnerships, and high-quality visuals that make people stop scrolling. Unlike traditional STRs, glamping attracts a niche audience that's after memorable, experience-driven stays. This chapter will walk you through the exact strategies to connect with that audience, convert browsers into bookers, and give your brand the rocket boost it needs to rise above the competition.

Brand Development

Branding is the foundation of any marketing strategy. A strong, memorable brand sets a glamping site apart in an increasingly competitive market. Guests are drawn to unique stays with compelling narratives, making it essential to define a clear identity that resonates with your target audience.

The first step in brand development is crafting a compelling story. Travelers who choose glamping aren't just looking for a place to sleep—they're looking for an experience. Your brand should reflect the essence of your location, the inspiration behind your accommodations, and the type of experience guests can expect. Whether your site is an off-grid escape, a luxury eco-retreat, or a family-friendly adventure spot, your brand should highlight what makes your property one of a kind.

Next, visual branding plays a crucial role in shaping guest perceptions. A cohesive logo, color palette, font selection, and overall aesthetic should be consistent across all platforms, including your website, social media, and promotional materials. A well-designed brand creates instant recognition and trust among potential guests.

Additionally, defining a brand voice is critical. Whether your tone is adventurous, playful, romantic, or luxurious, your messaging should be consistent across all communication channels. This voice should be reflected in everything from website copy to Instagram captions and email marketing campaigns. A well-crafted brand builds loyalty, increases direct bookings, and positions your glamping business as a destination rather than just a place to stay.

A high-converting website is one of the most powerful tools for marketing a glamping site. Many travelers prefer to book directly rather than through third-party platforms like Airbnb or Vrbo, especially if they can find exclusive offers or added perks. Your website must be designed to showcase your accommodations, tell your brand story, and guide visitors seamlessly through the booking process.

The first priority is user experience (UX). A poorly designed or slow-loading website will cause potential guests to leave before making a reservation. The website should be mobile friendly, easy to navigate, and visually appealing, ensuring that potential guests can quickly find the information they need.

Key website elements include:

- **High-quality visuals**: Large, professional photos of accommodations, outdoor spaces, and nearby attractions.
- **Detailed descriptions**: Engaging text that highlights amenities, unique experiences, and what makes your glamping site special.
- **An integrated booking system**: A seamless reservation process with a secure payment gateway to encourage direct bookings.
- **SEO-optimized content**: Blog posts, FAQs, and location-specific pages that improve search engine rankings and attract organic traffic.
- **Testimonials and reviews**: Social proof from past guests to build trust with new visitors.

SEO is a crucial aspect of website optimization. Researching and using keywords like "glamping in Texas," "luxury camping near [xyz city]," or "best eco-friendly stays in [xyz state]" helps your site rank higher in search results. Regularly updating content with blogs about local attractions, seasonal events, and travel guides also boosts visibility and establishes your site as an authority in the niche. There are several tools that can help identify your SEO rankings and where to improve your website.

Social Media Management

Social Media Platforms You Should Know & What Type of Content They Use	
Instagram	Short-form videos (reels), photos (carousels)
TikTok	Short-form videos, photos (carousels)
YouTube	Long-form videos
YouTube Shorts	Short-form videos
Facebook Business Page	Short-form videos (reels), photos (Carousels)

Social media is one of the most effective ways to engage potential guests and build a loyal following. Platforms like Instagram, TikTok, and Facebook are especially powerful for glamping businesses because they rely heavily on visual storytelling. We consistently ask guests where they heard about us, and 60–70 percent of the responses say from social media. Another 20 percent is from an OTA (usually Airbnb), and the rest varies from word of mouth or print media. Here are some tips to effectively leverage social media for your glamping business.

- **Consistency and engagement:** Posting consistently keeps your brand top of mind for potential guests. A mix of high-quality photos, short-form videos, guest testimonials, and behind-the-scenes content helps maintain engagement. Responding to comments and messages quickly also boosts credibility and fosters community.
- **Content themes and posting schedule:** Rotating through content themes can make planning easier. For example:
    - **Mondays**: "Meet the Host" or property updates
    - **Wednesdays**: "Guest Stories" featuring user-generated content

- **Fridays**: Travel guides or local recommendations
- **Sundays**: Booking promotions and discounts
- **Leveraging short-form video**: TikTok and Instagram Reels are excellent platforms for showcasing your site in an engaging way. Videos like "A Day at Our Glamping Site," "Guest Reactions Upon Arrival," and "Behind-the-Scenes of Our Most Popular Cabin" perform well and increase brand exposure.

Social media isn't just a place to showcase your glamping site—it's a powerful tool for driving direct bookings. However, getting engagement is one thing; turning that engagement into paying guests is another. Here's how you can leverage call to actions (CTAs), contests, and algorithm-friendly content to grow your audience and convert them into bookings.

A strong CTA guides potential guests toward the next step—whether that's booking a stay, inquiring about availability, or signing up for a discount. The key is to create CTAs that are simple, engaging, and frictionless.

Examples of high-converting CTAs include:

- **"Comment 'GLAMPING' for a discount code!"**: Encourages interaction while making guests feel like they're getting an exclusive deal. You can automate responses using tools like ManyChat to instantly send discount codes via DMs.
- **"DM us 'BOOK' to get available dates and special pricing!":** Directs interested users into a conversation where you can close the sale.
- **"Swipe up to book now!" (on Instagram stories)**: Removes extra steps and leads people straight to your booking page.
- **"Tag a friend who needs a getaway!"**: Encourages organic word-of-mouth marketing.

Why it works:

- **Boosts engagement.** More comments, shares, and DMs increase your post's reach in social media algorithms.
- **Creates a sense of urgency.** A time-limited offer or exclusive deal makes people act fast.

- **Simplifies the booking process.** Guests don't need to click around or search for your site; they're guided directly to the next step. Hosting a contest is one of the fastest ways to boost engagement, grow your following, and get potential guests talking about your property. People love free experiences, and a well-structured contest can make your brand go viral.

One of the guaranteed ways to get engagement is launching a giveaway for your site. You can run this on your own social media pages, but if you are a rather small presence or just starting out, consider partnering with an influencer for this type of promotion.

- **Choose an irresistible prize.** A free night's stay or an exclusive glamping experience is ideal.
- **Make entry simple.** The fewer steps, the better. Example: "Follow us, like this post, and tag two friends in the comments to enter!"
- **Encourage shares.** Require participants to share the post to their stories for an extra entry.
- **Collect user-generated content (UGC).** Ask participants to post a picture or video of their past camping/glamping experiences with a branded hashtag to increase visibility.

Example Giveaway Post:

GIVEAWAY ALERT!
Want to escape into nature for a FREE luxury glamping stay?
Here's how to enter:

Follow @YourGlampingSite
Like this post

Tag two friends who would love to go glamping with you! (Each comment = 1 entry)
Bonus Entry: Share this post to your story and tag us!

Giveaway ends [insert date]. Winner will be announced in our stories!

Why it works:

- **Rapid follower growth.** More people engage, and the algorithm pushes your content to even more users.
- **Word-of-mouth marketing.** Tagged friends become potential guests who learn about your site.
- **Creates buzz and FOMO.** People don't want to miss out on a free stay.

Social media is an interest-based algorithm—meaning platforms prioritize content that keeps people engaged. If your posts aren't performing well, it's likely because they're not triggering enough interaction (likes, comments, shares, saves).

How to Create Engaging Content

- **Study what works.** Look at your competitors' most successful posts and reverse engineer them. What type of content is getting them the most views, likes, and comments?
- **Use viral video trends.** If there's a trending sound or format that aligns with your brand, jump on it early.
- **Post shareable content.** Behind-the-scenes tours, glamping hacks, funny guest reactions, and breathtaking drone footage perform well.
- **Encourage conversation.** Ask questions, create polls, and use interactive stickers in stories.
- **Leverage guest content.** Encourage past guests to tag your location so you can repost their experiences.

Example Post Ideas That Get Engagement

- "What's your ideal glamping setup? Comment below: A) Tree house 🜂 B) Dome 🜁 C) Cabin 🏠" (Encourages comments)
- "POV: You just arrived at your dream glamping stay" (Show arrival experience with trending audio)
- "3 things you didn't know about glamping" (Short, snappy facts that keep people watching)

- "Would you stay here? 😎" (Show off your property with an epic video—gets shares and saves)

Why it works:

- **Higher engagement** = **more reach.** The more people interact, the more the algorithm promotes your content.
- **More visibility** = **more bookings.** Increased exposure puts your property in front of potential guests.
- **Proven strategies** = **faster growth.** Instead of guessing, mimic what's already working in the industry.

Content marketing is essential for long-term visibility and organic traffic. Creating valuable, shareable content helps establish your brand as a go-to glamping destination.

Writing SEO-friendly blogs not only attracts organic traffic but also educates potential guests. Blog topics should cater to your audience's interests, such as:

- **"The Best Time to Visit Our Glamping Site"**
- **"Top 10 Things to Do Near [Your Location]"**
- **"A Weekend Itinerary for the Ultimate Glamping Getaway"**
- **"Eco-Friendly Travel: How Our Glamping Site Reduces Its Environmental Impact"**

Each post should include stunning images, internal links to booking pages, and a strong CTA directing readers to reserve their stay.

Another content marketing strategy is email newsletters. A well-crafted monthly email keeps past and potential guests engaged. Topics might include:

- Exclusive discounts for repeat guests.
- Seasonal travel inspiration.
- Upcoming local events that align with glamping experiences.

High-quality photography is nonnegotiable for a successful glamping business. Since guests make booking decisions based on visuals, your content must be professionally shot and capture the full experience. The good ones aren't cheap, and the cheap ones aren't good, just to be frank. You can find some reasonable ones with good quality within the $200–500 range, but the top-tier photographers will run you at least $1,000 and up.

Investing in professional photography and drone footage can dramatically improve your marketing materials. Your images should highlight:

- Interior and exterior shots of each accommodation.
- Outdoor scenery, especially during golden hour.
- Lifestyle shots of guests enjoying firepits, hot tubs, or outdoor dining spaces.
- Close-ups of design details that make your site unique.

In addition to still photography, video content—such as 360-degree tours, time-lapse sunsets, and slow-motion shots of cozy campfires—can enhance your visual storytelling. UGC is also invaluable. Encouraging guests to tag your social media accounts in their posts provides free marketing and authentic endorsements.

Influencer Partnerships

Collaborating with influencers is an effective way to reach new audiences. Glamping attracts travel bloggers, adventure influencers, and lifestyle content creators who are always looking for unique places to stay. Content creators in years past were almost guaranteed to make content in exchange for just a free stay. As time has passed, creators have become more popular and business forward. Every city and creator is different, but this chart provides an estimate from what I have typically seen in Texas in particular. I have worked with over one hundred creators now and have spent at least $10,000-plus.

Typical Influencer Pay Rates	
Number of Followers	**Benefits**
0–10,000	Free stay exchange
10,000–50,000	Free stay exchange and $0–$500
50,000–100,000	Free stay exchange and $0–$1,000
100,000–500,000	Free stay exchange and $500–$2,000
500,000+	Free stay exchange and $1,000–$5,000+

It is important to understand that the biggest sign that a creator will be successful is not their follower count but their quality of content and target audience. I have had smaller creators (5,000–15,000 followers) create some of my most viral videos. I have also paid big-time creators (300,000+ followers) and the videos performed terribly. The social media algorithms are sometimes a crapshoot, and your chances increase by working with more creators making quality content.

I use Instagram as a major source of finding creators. I will search through hashtags such "Houston foodie," "Texas travel," "Texas things to do," and other similar ideas. I also will look at competing area properties and see who they have used. I look for travel vloggers first in particular, but I have found that the "foodie" or "food review" sections are equally as valuable. The overlap in the hospitality review world seems to be the biggest reason they also make great "place to stay" content.

When choosing influencers, focus on those whose audience aligns with your ideal guests. A micro-influencer (5,000–50,000 followers) with high engagement rates and a niche audience is often more valuable than a mega-influencer with a broad but disengaged following. If you watch some of their videos and instantly think *Wow, what cool videos*, other people on social media will likely think the same.

Effective influencer campaigns include:

- **Press stays**: Hosting an influencer in exchange for social media posts and blog features.
- **Affiliate partnerships**: Providing a discount code where influencers earn a small commission for every booking made through their link.
- **Collaborative content**: Having an influencer take over your Instagram for a day or contribute to your blog.

An influencer marketing strategy should be measured for ROI by tracking booking increases, engagement levels, and social media growth after each collaboration. Marketing can sometimes come down to cost benefits, and knowing how valuable an influencer stay is matters. If you are spending $500 on paid advertising (Meta, TikTok, Google, etc.) and spending $500 on cleaning fees after free influencer exchange stays, you'll need to know which one is actually working.

Is Your Marketing Actually Working?

Marketing can either be a bottomless money pit or a booking machine—it all depends on whether you track the right metrics. Understanding what's driving reservations (and what's wasting money) is key to optimizing your efforts. Here's how to measure success across different channels.

Social media can be a powerful tool, but if you don't track results, you won't know if your content is actually translating into bookings. The best way to measure performance is by assigning unique discount codes to different platforms and influencers.

- Example: Use "Insta10" for Instagram and "TikTok10" for TikTok to give guests 10 percent off direct bookings. This allows you to see which platform is generating more reservations.
- Provide influencers with custom codes, so you can track exactly who is bringing in paying customers.

Beyond promo codes, pay attention to key engagement metrics.

- **Accounts reached and accounts engaged.** Are your posts reaching new audiences, or are you just talking to the same followers?
- **Follower growth.** More followers means more potential guests—but only if they're engaged.
- **Demographics (age, location, interests).** Are you reaching travelers who actually fit your target guest profile?

Running ads on Google, Meta (Facebook and Instagram), and travel sites can drive direct bookings—but only if they're optimized. Tracking the right metrics ensures you're getting an ROI.

Key metrics to watch:

- **Cost per click (CPC):** How much are you paying for each person who clicks your ad? Lower CPC generally means more efficient spending.
- **Click-through rate (CTR):** What percentage of people actually click your ad after seeing it? A low CTR means your ad needs better visuals, copy, or targeting.

- **Cost per booking (CPB):** The most important metric—how much does it cost to acquire a paying guest? If your CPB is too high, you're burning money.
- **Return on ad spend (ROAS):** Are you making more money than you're spending? A ROAS of at least 3:1 ($3 in revenue for every $1 spent) is a good benchmark.
- **Conversion rate:** How many clicks actually turn into bookings? If this number is low, your website or booking process might need optimization.

Key Engagement and Advertising Metrics for STRs

Category	Metric	What to Watch For	Why It Matters
Social Media Engagement	Accounts Reached	Are you reaching *new* audiences, not just existing followers?	Expands your potential guest pool.
	Accounts Engaged	Are people actually interacting (likes, comments, shares)?	Shows content relevance and connection.
Social Media Engagement	Follower Growth	Are you gaining *engaged* new followers?	More engaged followers = more future guests.
	Demographics	Are your followers the *right* travelers? (age, location, interests)	Targets your ideal guest, not randoms.
	Cost Per Click (CPC)	How much you're paying per click. Lower = better.	Measures ad spending efficiency.
	Click-Through Rate (CTR)	Percentage of people who click after seeing your ad.	Tests ad appeal and targeting quality.
Advertising Metrics	Cost Per Booking (CPB)	Cost to actually get a paying guest.	True cost to grow your bookings.
	Return on Ad Spend (ROAS)	Revenue earned for every dollar spent. Aim for at least 3:1.	Ensures your ads are profitable, not wasteful.
	Conversion Rate	Percentage of clicks that turn into bookings.	Tests your website and booking flow.

Final Thoughts

A well-executed marketing strategy is the key to a thriving glamping business. By developing a compelling brand, optimizing your website, leveraging social media, investing in high-quality visuals, and collaborating with influencers, you can position your glamping site as a sought-after destination. Consistency, authenticity, and engagement are the driving forces behind successful marketing. With the right strategies in place, your glamping site can attract adventure seekers, nature lovers, and experience-driven travelers looking for an unforgettable stay.

Lessons from the Field

- **Branding matters.** A strong story and visuals build trust.
- **Optimize your website.** Fast, SEO-friendly sites convert more bookings.
- **Social media sells.** Engaging content and videos attract guests.
- **Content drives traffic.** Blogs and newsletters bring long-term growth.
- **Quality visuals convert.** Pro photos and guest content boost bookings.
- **Influencers expand reach.** Micro-influencers drive awareness and trust.
- **Stay consistent.** A multichannel strategy keeps your site competitive.

Chapter 12

Distribution and Sales

In today's fast-moving travel landscape, glamping isn't just about offering a one-of-a-kind outdoor experience—it's about making sure your ideal guest knows you exist and can easily book with you. When we first launched, nearly all our bookings came through Airbnb. But after implementing the marketing strategies covered in the previous chapter, we quickly realized the power and profitability of diversifying. Today, 60–70 percent of our bookings are direct, and we consistently generate revenue through five or more different channels. While Airbnb remains a dominant force, emerging platforms are gaining ground—and ignoring them means leaving money on the table.

As the glamping space grows more competitive, a strong multichannel strategy is no longer optional—it's essential. In this chapter, we'll break down the key distribution platforms and sales tactics you need to know, from direct booking systems and OTAs to pricing strategies, yield management, package offerings, and group sales for events or retreats. By the end, you'll have a clear road map to drive more bookings, increase revenue, and create a resilient business built for long-term success.

Direct Booking Systems

The Importance of Direct Bookings

Direct booking systems allow glamping operators to accept reservations through their own websites or dedicated booking portals without relying on third-party intermediaries. Property management systems (PMS) like Hospitable allows you to easily build your own direct booking system that integrates seamlessly with your operation. This direct channel is particularly attractive because it offers higher profit margins by eliminating OTA commission fees—often 15–25 percent—and enables operators to cultivate direct relationships with their guests.

Investing in a professional, user-friendly website is the cornerstone of a successful direct booking system. PMS can often allow you to build a website with templates they provide. These are great to get started in the direct booking world and offer a user-friendly way for building for hosts who typically lack the expertise needed to build a website from the ground up. These websites often have great integrations but do lack the "wow factor" and functionality of a more polished design.

Once you have tested out a simpler website design and are ready to take your direct bookings to the next level, your best option will be joining forces with a custom website builder. You can find some DIY options, such as Wix and Squarespace, that have some well-designed templates, but I recommend hiring someone who builds websites professionally.

PMS like Hospitable will allow you to take widgets or their public API from their software interface and have a professional designer implement these onto a custom-built website. There are several choices on what type of platform to allow the website designer to build on (WordPress, Wix, Squarespace, etc.), and researching the pros and cons of each will allow you to make informed decisions.

Here are some key components to consider:

- **Responsive design and user experience:** Your website should be mobile-friendly and easy to navigate. A clean design, fast load times, and a seamless booking process are essential. The more frictionless the experience, the higher your conversion rates.
- **Integrated booking engine:** An integrated booking engine allows guests to check availability, view rates, and book their stay directly. Many platforms offer solutions tailored to the hospitality industry. These systems often include built-in payment processing, calendar synchronization, and automated confirmation emails.
- **Search engine optimization (SEO):** Optimize your website content with relevant keywords (e.g., "luxury glamping," "eco-friendly camping") to improve your search engine rankings. Higher visibility on search engines drives organic traffic, which can translate into more direct bookings.
- **Email marketing and social media integration:** Collect guest emails during the booking process and use them for targeted marketing campaigns. Share special offers, seasonal updates, and exclusive packages to nurture repeat business. Additionally, integrating social media platforms can help promote your brand and drive traffic back to your website.

While direct bookings can significantly boost your bottom line, they require a sustained investment in digital marketing, technology, and customer relationship management. You'll need to balance the initial costs against long-term gains in customer loyalty and reduced dependency on third parties. Remember, there are extra costs associated with direct bookings such as payment processing, guest verification, website maintenance, marketing expenses, and more. Controlling the guest experience from start to finish and being able to build your direct customer database is a crucial part of hospitality, though, and with the right steps, a direct booking system can be a game changer.

Online Travel Agencies (OTAs)

Online travel agencies (OTAs) like Airbnb, Booking.com, Expedia, and Vrbo have revolutionized the travel industry by offering consumers a convenient way to discover and book accommodations. For glamping operators, OTAs provide immediate access to a vast audience of travelers actively seeking unique lodging experiences.

To harness the full potential of OTAs, consider the following strategies:

- **Optimize your listings:** High-quality photos, engaging descriptions, and accurate amenity details are critical to capturing potential guests' attention. Regularly update your listing to reflect seasonal offerings and any improvements to your property.
- **Dynamic pricing and promotions:** OTAs often provide tools for dynamic pricing, allowing you to adjust rates based on demand, seasonality, and local events. Offering limited-time promotions or discounts can also help boost visibility and drive bookings.
- **Leverage reviews and ratings:** Encourage satisfied guests to leave positive reviews, as these significantly influence booking decisions. Monitor and respond to reviews—both positive and negative—to show that you value guest feedback and are committed to providing exceptional experiences.
- **Maintain rate parity:** Many OTAs require rate parity, meaning your direct booking rates should be comparable to those listed on OTA platforms. Balancing direct and

OTA rates can be challenging, but maintaining consistency is key to preserving your brand integrity and guest trust.

While OTAs offer an impressive reach and convenience, they also come with significant challenges. High commission fees and limited control over customer data are just the beginning. These platforms can change their rules, algorithms, and policies at a moment's notice, potentially impacting your property's visibility and revenue without warning. Worse yet, hosts can face bans or suspensions based on false guest complaints or misunderstandings within the OTA's review system, leaving you vulnerable to unpredictable disruptions.

Moreover, you're often at the mercy of the OTA's review mechanisms and customer support teams, which may not prioritize your concerns or resolve issues promptly. This lack of control over your online reputation can be particularly damaging, as a single negative review can skew ratings and deter potential guests. For these reasons, it's wise to integrate OTAs into a broader distribution mix, building your own direct booking pipeline to maintain control, reduce dependency, and ensure a more stable revenue stream.

Pricing Strategies

Pricing is a critical lever in revenue management, influencing both occupancy and profitability. In the glamping industry, pricing strategies must account for seasonal fluctuations, competitive landscapes, and the unique value proposition of your property.

Dynamic pricing involves adjusting your rates in real time, based on market demand, booking trends, and competitor pricing. Several software tools, such as PriceLabs, Beyond Pricing, and Wheelhouse, can automate these adjustments, ensuring that your property remains competitive while maximizing revenue. According to OnRes, dynamic pricing strategies can boost revenue by up to 10–20 percent in the hospitality industry.[5]

One of the foundational tools in dynamic pricing is base price optimization. This feature allows you to set a dynamic base price that adapts to market trends, demand fluctuations, and seasonal variations. Studying other comparable listings to suggest an optimal starting point for yourself and using dynamic pricing softwares understanding of

---

[5] Steve Behrisch, "Maximizing Hotel Profits: The Role of Technology in Pricing Strategy," *The OnRes Blog*, 23 May 2024, https://www.onressoftware.com/impact-of-technology-on-hotel-pricing/.

the market can help you setr this. Whether you choose a market-based positioning at the 25th, 50th, or 75th percentile of the local market, an imported base price for new listings, or even a custom base price you will be able to experiment and use data to help your decision. Regularly revisiting and tweaking this base price using features like base price nudges can keep your property competitive throughout the year.

Beyond the base rate, paying attention to Length of Stay (LOS) pricing adjustments enables you to apply percentage changes based on the duration of a guest's stay. For example, you might incentivize longer stays with a 10 percent discount for week-long bookings or a 20 percent discount for two-week reservations. This adjustment sits on top of other customizations, ensuring that every booking reflects the ideal balance between occupancy and revenue.

For properties in highly seasonal markets or those with unique demand patterns, custom seasonal profiles allow you to set minimum and maximum prices for specific date ranges and even adjust minimum stay requirements. This gives you the flexibility to manage pricing during peak seasons or local events more proactively. Similarly, day-of-the-week pricing adjustments let you fine-tune your rates based on daily trends; if your property sees higher demand on weekdays for corporate travelers, you can adjust prices by a specific percentage to capture that extra value.

Another layer of customization is provided by the demand factor, which lets you adjust how responsive your pricing algorithm is to daily demand trends—particularly during holidays or special events. You can choose from conservative, recommended, or aggressive settings to fine-tune how much your rates should fluctuate based on transient market conditions.

Minimum Length of Stay customization and adjacent day/orphan day discounts further refine your strategy. By setting minimum stay requirements based on market data, you ensure that each booking meets your revenue and occupancy targets. Meanwhile, adjusting prices for orphan days (gaps between bookings) or for adjacent days encourages guests to book consecutively, reducing vacancies and optimizing revenue across the board.

In essence, these customizations provide a granular level of control over your pricing strategy. They allow you to respond quickly to changing market conditions while maintaining a clear, data-driven approach to revenue management. By leveraging these tools, property managers can not only maximize occupancy but also ensure that every booked night contributes optimally to your bottom line—all while staying ahead of the competition in an increasingly dynamic short-term rental market.

Psychological pricing techniques play a vital role in influencing consumer behavior in the hospitality industry. One common method is charm pricing—setting rates just below a round number (e.g., $199 instead of $200)—which takes advantage of the left-digit effect, making prices appear significantly lower than they actually are. This technique is often complemented by bundling services or experiences, such as including complimentary breakfast, spa credits, or guided tours with your room rate, which enhances the perceived value of the offering. Bundled packages not only differentiate your property from competitors but also simplify decision-making for potential guests by presenting a comprehensive experience at a single, attractive price.

Other effective psychological pricing strategies include anchoring and decoy pricing. With anchoring, a higher "original" price is displayed next to the discounted rate, which helps establish a reference point that makes the discount seem more substantial. Decoy pricing involves offering multiple pricing tiers, where one option is intentionally made less attractive to steer customers toward a more profitable middle option. Additionally, some hotels use tiered pricing models that provide different levels of service and amenities, ensuring that guests feel they have choices that align with their budget and preferences. By carefully crafting these pricing strategies, hospitality providers can subtly guide customer perceptions and decision-making, ultimately leading to increased bookings and higher overall revenue.

Yield Management

Yield management is the practice of optimizing revenue by adjusting pricing based on real-time demand and occupancy data. It's a strategy commonly used in the airline and hotel industries, and it can be equally effective for glamping operations.

- **Demand forecasting:** Analyzing historical booking data, local events, and seasonal trends helps predict demand fluctuations. This enables you to adjust pricing in advance to capitalize on periods of high demand or mitigate the impact of slow periods.

- **Inventory control:** Managing the number of available units and reservation restrictions during high-demand periods can help maximize revenue. For instance, offering minimum stay requirements during peak seasons can increase overall profitability.
- **Technology and tools:** Yield management software can automate much of this process. Tools like Beyond Pricing and Wheelhouse analyze data in real time and suggest rate adjustments to optimize revenue.

For glamping operators, yield management may involve adjusting rates not only for nightly stays but also for packages and add-on services. Special events, weekends, and holidays can be targeted with premium pricing, while slower periods may see discounts or value-added packages to attract bookings.

Package Development

Package development is about bundling your glamping accommodations with additional experiences or services to create a more attractive and differentiated offering. Packages can enhance the guest experience and drive higher average revenue per booking.

- **Adventure and experience bundles.** Combine your lodging with outdoor activities like guided hikes, kayaking, or zip-lining. These experiences add value and appeal to guests looking for a complete adventure.
- **Wellness retreats.** Bundle your glamping stay with wellness activities such as yoga sessions, meditation workshops, and spa treatments. Wellness tourism is a growing trend, and offering a holistic experience can attract health-conscious travelers.
- **Seasonal and themed packages.** Develop packages that align with seasonal events or local festivals. For example, a "Fall Foliage Retreat" could include scenic drives, local culinary experiences, and nature walks.

Partnering with local businesses can be a game changer for your package offerings, providing guests with an enriched, authentic experience that goes far beyond just a place to sleep. For instance, collaborating with nearby wineries can allow you to offer exclusive wine tastings or vineyard tours that perfectly complement your glamping experience, while partnering with local restaurants can secure your guests special dining discounts or even a curated farm-to-table meal. By working together, both your glamping site and the local business benefit from increased exposure and a more diversified revenue stream.

These partnerships foster a sense of community and authenticity that today's travelers crave. When you bundle exclusive experiences—like guided hikes with a local adventure tour company or cultural tours with a neighborhood guide—your guests receive a well-rounded, memorable stay that they can't get anywhere else. Joint marketing initiatives, such as co-branded promotions and social media shout-outs, further amplify your reach, tapping into the local business's customer base while building lasting relationships that encourage repeat bookings and long-term success.

Once you've developed attractive packages, effective marketing is key. Use your direct booking website, OTA listings, and social media channels to promote these bundles. High-quality visuals and compelling descriptions can help convey the value of your package, enticing potential guests to choose your property over competitors.

Group Sales and Corporate Retreats

While individual bookings are important, group sales and corporate retreats offer a significant opportunity for glamping operators. These segments often command premium pricing and can lead to extended stays and repeat business.

- **Higher occupancy rates:** Group bookings generally fill more of your available capacity in a single reservation, reducing the risk of unoccupied nights.
- **Premium revenue:** Corporate retreats and group events are willing to pay a premium for unique, memorable experiences that serve as team-building exercises or incentive trips.
- **Brand exposure:** osting corporate events can enhance your brand's reputation and visibility. Satisfied corporate clients may return with new bookings or refer others to your property.
- **Tailored offerings:** Develop packages specifically for corporate retreats, including meeting spaces, team-building activities, and catering options. Ensure that your property

can comfortably accommodate larger groups without compromising the intimate glamping experience.
- **Networking and partnerships:** Connect with local event planners, corporate travel agents, and business associations. Attending industry conferences and trade shows can also help you forge valuable relationships that drive group bookings.
- **Flexible pricing models:** Offer tiered pricing options for group bookings, such as volume discounts for larger parties or longer stays. This flexibility can make your offering more attractive to corporate clients who are balancing budget constraints with the desire for quality experiences.
- **Showcase success stories:** Leverage testimonials, case studies, and high-quality visuals from previous group events or retreats. Sharing real-world examples of successful events can build trust and encourage new bookings.

Digital marketing isn't just for individual consumers—it's also a powerful tool for B2B (business-to-business) sales. Consider these tactics:

- **LinkedIn marketing:** Use LinkedIn to target corporate decision-makers and event planners. Regular posts, sponsored content, and targeted ads can help raise awareness of your group packages.
- **Email campaigns:** Develop a dedicated email campaign for corporate clients. Highlight the unique features of your glamping property, special corporate packages, and any seasonal promotions designed for group events.
- **Content marketing:** Create blog posts, white papers, or videos that showcase how glamping can serve as an ideal venue for corporate retreats. Providing valuable content can position you as an expert in the niche, building credibility and attracting potential clients.

Successful glamping operators don't rely solely on one distribution channel. Instead, they adopt a multichannel strategy that blends direct bookings, OTA listings, dynamic pricing, and specialized packages to create a resilient and adaptable revenue model. This approach ensures that you can capture demand from various segments while maintaining control over your brand and profitability.

Leveraging data is critical when managing distribution and sales. Use analytics tools to track booking sources, monitor occupancy trends, and evaluate the performance of different pricing strategies. Tools like Google Analytics, OTA dashboards, and yield management software can provide valuable insights to fine-tune your strategy. By analyzing data regularly, you can make informed decisions that enhance both revenue and guest satisfaction.

While OTAs and dynamic pricing tools can drive short-term bookings, investing in direct booking systems and personalized guest experiences builds long-term brand loyalty. It's a balancing act—using OTAs to reach a broader audience while nurturing direct relationships that lead to repeat business. A hybrid strategy ensures that you capture immediate revenue opportunities while establishing a sustainable foundation for future growth.

Final Thoughts

In the competitive world of glamping, a well-rounded distribution and sales strategy is not just an operational necessity—it's a key driver of success. By harnessing the power of direct booking systems, optimizing your presence on OTAs, implementing dynamic pricing and yield management, and crafting compelling packages for both individual and group bookings, you can significantly boost your revenue while delivering unforgettable guest experiences.

Lessons from the Field

- **Direct bookings maximize profit.** A strong website and marketing strategy reduce reliance on OTAs.
- **OTAs offer reach but limit control.** Use them wisely while building your direct booking pipeline.
- **Dynamic pricing increases revenue.** Tools like PriceLabs help adjust rates based on demand.
- **Packages boost value.** Bundling stays with experiences increases bookings and guest satisfaction.
- **Corporate retreats are lucrative.** Group sales bring premium revenue and repeat business.

- **Multichannel strategy wins.** Combining OTAs, direct bookings, and strategic pricing creates stability.
- **Data drives success.** Track trends, analyze booking sources, and optimize strategies for long-term growth.

Chapter 13

Customer Relationship Management

Earlier, I mentioned the guest who sat in a broken outdoor chair—and how I still managed to turn that experience into a five-star review. Here's exactly how it happened.

It started with empathy. I asked myself, *How would I feel if this happened to me?* Probably embarrassed. Definitely annoyed with the property. So I immediately apologized, but more importantly, I asked one simple question: How can I make this right for you? That small gesture made a big impact—it showed the guest I wasn't just sorry; I was committed to making it right. He appreciated the effort and told me not to worry, but I didn't stop there.

I recommended one of my favorite local restaurants and offered to buy them dinner via delivery, just to go the extra mile. I also reassured him that we'd take immediate steps to prevent anything like that from happening again. In the end, not only did he leave us a five-star review and highlight how we handled the situation, but he also returned later to stay at another one of my tiny homes. That moment reminded me that mistakes happen—but how you respond is what guests remember.

In the fiercely competitive world of hospitality, customer relationship management (CRM) is no longer just an operational add-on—it's a strategic imperative. Effective CRM is about building and nurturing long-term relationships with your guests, ensuring that every interaction—from the first inquiry to the post-stay follow-up—creates value and fosters loyalty. This chapter delves into key components of a robust CRM strategy for glamping and short-term rental operators, including building customer loyalty, managing reviews, collecting and implementing feedback, leveraging email marketing, and developing repeat guest programs. We'll also explore the role of automation in streamlining these processes, such as using auto-messages to ask for reviews and sending automated check-in messages to gather private feedback before minor issues turn into major problems.

By the end of this chapter, you'll understand how to transform your guest interactions into long-term relationships that drive repeat business, generate positive online reviews, and ultimately boost your bottom line.

The Keys to a 5 Star Guest Experience	
Flawless cleanliness	Ensure spotless units with photo-verified cleaning.
Seamless check-in	Use smart locks and clear instructions.
Fast response times	Reply to guests quickly via AI messaging or VAs.
Personal touches	Welcome notes, s'mores kits, or local recommendations.
Comfort and convenience	High-quality bedding, strong Wi-Fi, and hot showers.
Proactive maintenance	Fix issues before guests notice.
Clear communication	Send pre-arrival and post-stay messages.
Encourage reviews	Encourage reviews.
Exceed expectations	Surprise upgrades or thoughtful gestures.
Follow up	Respond to reviews and show you value guest feedback.

Building Customer Loyalty

The Importance of Loyalty in Hospitality

In the hospitality industry, customer loyalty is critical. Loyal guests are not only more likely to return, but they also become ambassadors for your brand, sharing positive experiences with friends, family, and online communities. Loyal customers tend to spend more, provide valuable feedback, and help buffer your business against market fluctuations.

One of the key strategies to build customer loyalty is personalization. Guests appreciate when their unique preferences are remembered and catered to. This might include remembering a guest's favorite room, offering personalized welcome amenities, or even addressing them by name in follow-up communications. Advanced CRM systems allow you to collect and analyze guest data, enabling you to tailor every aspect of the guest experience—from customized recommendations to exclusive offers that resonate with individual preferences.

Implementing a loyalty program can significantly enhance customer retention. Whether it's through a points-based system, exclusive discounts, or complimentary services, loyalty programs reward guests for choosing your property time and again. These programs can be integrated into your booking system, offering guests incentives such as early check-in, late checkout, or free upgrades. Some properties even offer a tiered loyalty program, where the benefits increase with each subsequent stay, providing a clear incentive for repeat business.

Customer loyalty is built over time through consistent engagement. It's not enough to simply deliver a great experience during the stay; you must continue to engage with your guests long after they leave. Social media platforms, personalized emails, and targeted promotions are all valuable tools for keeping your brand top of mind. A well-maintained CRM database enables you to segment your guests and send them tailored communications based on their past interactions and preferences.

Review Management

Online reviews are the lifeblood of the hospitality industry. They significantly influence potential guests' decisions and shape your property's reputation. Positive reviews can drive bookings, while negative reviews—even if unfounded—can harm your brand. This is why proactive review management is essential.

One effective way to boost positive reviews is by automating the process of asking for feedback. After a guest's stay, automated messages can be sent out to request reviews. These messages should be friendly, personalized, and timely. For example, an automated email or SMS sent shortly after checkout—when the experience is still fresh—can gently encourage guests to share their thoughts on platforms like Google, TripAdvisor, or Airbnb. The key is to strike a balance: You want to remind guests without coming across as pushy.

An innovative strategy for managing reviews is to proactively ask for feedback via an automated check-in message on the night of arrival. This message can serve two critical purposes. First, it offers a direct line of communication with the guest to ensure that everything is going smoothly. Second, it provides an opportunity to gather private feedback before any issues escalate and before the guest is prompted to leave a public review. By addressing concerns in real time, you can often resolve issues quietly and improve the overall guest experience, which in turn can lead to more positive reviews later on.

For example, you might send a message such as:

> *Hi [Guest Name], we hope you're enjoying your stay so far! We'd love to hear if everything is going well or if there's anything we can improve. Feel free to reply directly to this message—your comfort is our top priority."*

This kind of proactive approach not only helps mitigate potential negative feedback but also demonstrates your commitment to guest satisfaction.

Automated systems can also alert you when new reviews are posted, allowing you to respond promptly. A timely, well-crafted response to both positive and negative reviews can go a long way in enhancing your reputation. Acknowledge positive reviews with gratitude, and address negative reviews with empathy and a plan for resolution. This responsiveness shows potential guests that you care about their experience and are committed to making improvements when needed.

Feedback Collection and Implementation

Collecting guest feedback is crucial for understanding what's working and what needs improvement. It provides insights into your property's strengths and weaknesses and helps guide strategic decisions. While public reviews are valuable, private feedback is even more critical because it can reveal issues that guests might not feel comfortable posting online. By gathering detailed feedback, you can continuously refine your service and address concerns before they become widespread problems.

Automated messaging systems are incredibly effective for gathering feedback at key touchpoints. As mentioned earlier, sending an automated check-in message on the night of arrival allows you to capture immediate feedback. Similarly, a follow-up message at checkout can ask for an overall rating of the stay, along with suggestions for improvement. These messages can be structured as short surveys or open-ended questions and should be designed to be as user-friendly as possible.

For instance, an automated checkout message might read:

> *Thank you for staying with us, [Guest Name]! We'd love to hear about your experience. Please let us know if there's anything we could have done better, or if you have any suggestions for future guests. Your feedback is invaluable in helping us improve.*

Many CRM and property management systems now integrate with survey tools and review platforms to streamline the feedback process. Software like GuestRevu, TrustYou, and even custom-built surveys can help collect and analyze feedback automatically. These tools often include analytics dashboards that help you identify trends and pinpoint recurring issues.

Collecting feedback is only half the battle—implementing changes based on that feedback is what truly sets a business apart. Establish a regular review process where feedback is analyzed and shared with relevant team members. Develop actionable plans to address common concerns and track the impact of any changes you make. This iterative process not only enhances the guest experience but also demonstrates to your customers that their opinions matter and lead to tangible improvements.

Email Marketing

We all get way too many emails, and figuring out how to stand out in the crowd can be challenging. You need to remember, though, that most adults check their email more frequently than they even check social media, and that trend is not going to change anytime soon. Email marketing remains one of the most powerful tools for maintaining an ongoing relationship with your guests. Unlike one-time communications, a well-crafted email campaign can keep your brand in front of past guests, encouraging them to book again or refer others to your property.

To maximize the impact of your email marketing, segmentation is key. Divide your email list into segments based on various criteria—such as previous booking behavior, location, interests, or even the type of property they stayed in. Personalized emails that speak directly to the recipient's preferences and past experiences are far more effective than generic blasts. For instance, if a guest previously booked a glamping site with a focus on outdoor adventure, you could send them a targeted email highlighting a new package that includes guided hiking or kayaking excursions.

Automation in email marketing can save time and ensure consistency. Tools like Mailchimp, Constant Contact, and HubSpot allow you to set up automated campaigns that send out welcome emails, post-stay thank-you messages, and periodic newsletters. An automated follow-up series can be particularly effective; after a guest's stay, you can schedule a sequence of emails that includes a thank-you note, a request for feedback, and a special discount offer for their next visit.

Beyond promotions and discounts, your emails should provide value to your guests. This could be in the form of travel tips, local event information, or exclusive insights into your property's updates and future offerings. By positioning your emails as a trusted source of relevant information rather than just sales pitches, you build a stronger, more enduring relationship with your audience.

It's essential to monitor the performance of your email marketing campaigns. Key metrics such as open rates, click-through rates, and conversion rates provide insights into what's working and what isn't. Use this data to continually refine your messaging, subject lines, and overall strategy. A/B testing different elements of your emails can help you optimize your approach and maximize engagement.

Repeat Guest Programs

I love all of my guests, but my favorite ones are truly repeat guests. It is much easier (and cheaper) to keep a customer than gain a new one, so finding ways to bring an already paying customer back is a top priority. Repeat guests are the cornerstone of a sustainable hospitality business. They not only generate consistent revenue but also tend to spend more over time, recommend your property to others, and require less marketing investment compared to acquiring new customers. Establishing a robust repeat guest program can help you capitalize on these benefits and build a loyal customer base.

One effective strategy is to offer exclusive incentives for returning guests. This could include special discounts, early access to new packages, or complimentary upgrades. For example, you might create a "returning guest discount" that offers a 15 percent discount on the next booking if the reservation is made within a year of their previous stay. These incentives not only encourage repeat bookings but also signal to guests that you value their loyalty.

Repeat guest programs work best when they are built on a foundation of detailed customer data. A robust CRM system can help you track guest preferences, past behaviors, and booking histories, enabling you to create highly personalized offers. For instance, if data shows that a particular guest consistently books a certain type of package or stays during a specific season, you can tailor communications and offers to match their behavior. This level of personalization makes guests feel understood and valued, increasing the likelihood that they will return.

Repeat guest programs should not be static; they need to evolve based on guest feedback and market trends. Regularly solicit feedback specifically from your repeat guests to understand what additional benefits or improvements they'd like to see. Use this feedback to adjust the program, whether it's by adding new perks, tweaking discount rates, or introducing entirely new membership tiers. This iterative approach ensures that your program remains relevant and continues to provide value over time.

Integrating Automation in CRM

Automation is a game changer when it comes to customer relationship management. Automated messaging can streamline many aspects of CRM, from gathering feedback to nurturing guest relationships. For example, sending automated check-in messages on the night of arrival can help you gauge a guest's initial impressions and identify any issues before they escalate. These messages can be programmed to request private feedback, ensuring that any problems are addressed promptly and discreetly—often preventing a negative review from surfacing later on.

In addition to check-in messages, automated review requests can significantly enhance your online reputation. Once a guest has checked out, a carefully crafted auto-message can invite them to leave a review. This message should express gratitude for their stay and encourage honest feedback. By automating this process, you ensure consistency and timeliness, which are key to capturing accurate reflections of the guest experience. Automation also takes the pressure off your team, allowing them to focus on resolving issues and enhancing the guest experience in real time.

The advantages of automated messaging extend beyond review requests. Proactive communication—such as automated follow-ups to ensure guests have everything they need—can help build a positive rapport with your guests. For instance, if a guest hasn't responded to a check-in message, a gentle reminder can show that you're committed to their satisfaction. This proactive approach can significantly reduce the chances of issues going unnoticed and demonstrates that your property cares about guest well-being.

Many modern property management systems (PMS) and CRM platforms now include robust automation features. Tools like Guest-Revu, Revinate, and even custom integrations with messaging apps can help you set up, monitor, and optimize your automated communications. These platforms often provide analytics that allows you to see which messages are driving engagement and where improvements can be made. By leveraging these tools, you can ensure that your CRM strategy is not only efficient but also highly effective at driving customer satisfaction and loyalty.

Customer relationship management is at the heart of a successful hospitality business. By investing in strategies that build loyalty, manage reviews, collect and act on feedback, nurture guest relationships through email marketing, and foster repeat business, you can create a robust and resilient operation that thrives even in competitive markets. Automation plays a pivotal role in this process, enabling you to capture valuable insights and respond to guest needs in real time—before issues escalate and affect your reputation.

From setting up automated messages, asking for reviews, and gathering private feedback through check-in communications to implementing segmented email campaigns and rewarding repeat guests with exclusive offers, every aspect of your CRM strategy should be designed to enhance the guest experience. The ultimate goal is to transform every guest interaction into an opportunity to build lasting relationships, driving both immediate bookings and long-term brand loyalty.

By leveraging advanced CRM systems and automation tools, you can not only streamline your operations but also gain a competitive edge in the market. Whether you're a small boutique glamping site or a larger hospitality enterprise, the strategies discussed in this chapter offer a road map to achieving superior customer satisfaction and sustained revenue growth. With a well-rounded CRM strategy, every guest can become a loyal customer and a powerful advocate for your brand—ensuring that your property stands out in a crowded marketplace and continues to thrive for years to come.

Final Thoughts

Effective customer relationship management (CRM) is the backbone of any successful hospitality business. From the moment a guest books to long after they check out, every interaction is a chance to elevate their experience, build trust, and create lasting loyalty. When done right, CRM isn't just about solving problems—it's about proactively shaping a guest journey that feels personal, seamless, and memorable.

By combining thoughtful automation with personalized communication, you can ensure guests feel seen and supported at every stage.

Invest in the right tools, pay attention to your data, and stay agile—adapting your strategy based on feedback and trends. These efforts won't just improve your day-to-day operations; they'll drive higher occupancy, repeat bookings, and long-term growth. A strong CRM strategy isn't optional—it's what sets thriving hospitality brands apart.

Lessons from the Field

- **Loyal guests = more profit.** A 5 percent increase in retention can boost profits by up to 20 percent.
- **Personalization wins.** Remember guest preferences, offer tailored experiences, and build loyalty.
- **Automate for efficiency.** Use auto-messages for check-ins, reviews, and feedback collection.
- **Manage reviews proactively.** Request positive reviews and address negative ones before they escalate.
- **Email marketing matters.** Segment lists, personalize messages, and nurture guest relationships.
- **Encourage repeat stays.** Offer discounts, VIP perks, and exclusive incentives for returning guests.

Part 5
Financial Management

Chapter 14

Financial Planning

Every glampreneur goes through a similar financial journey. At first, you're told how "cheap" it is to start a glamping business—and, like me, you might think, *Perfect, that's right up my alley*. But once you dig into the details, it quickly becomes clear that it's not as affordable as it sounds.

I fell victim to completely underestimating building my first geo dome. I figured it would be around $10,000 for the geo dome, and just adding utilities would be a simple straight-forward process. Maybe it would take $60,000, but I was sure I could get it down to $50,000. Boy, was I wrong.

In the beginning, it's easy to stay laser-focused on the present—just trying to get your build off the ground. You set a budget, feel confident, and then reality hits. Construction starts, costs climb, and suddenly that budget doesn't stretch as far as you thought. Somehow, you pull it off—scraping together funds, getting creative, and making it work.

You open your doors and start seeing cash flow, maybe even outperforming expectations if you've followed the marketing and operations strategies in this guide. But then the expenses start rolling in—and they're way higher than you anticipated. Eventually, you get a handle on both revenue and costs, but it becomes clear: You should have been planning for growth from day one. Without a financial strategy in place, it's easy to turn a promising business into a stressful cycle of unexpected costs and missed opportunities.

Financial planning is integral for any successful hospitality venture. In this chapter, we dive deep into the crucial aspects of financial management—from the initial start-up costs to detailed operating budgets, revenue forecasting, cash flow management, and the various financing options available. Whether you're launching a new glamping site, a boutique hotel, or any short-term rental property, understanding and implementing robust financial planning can be the difference between long-term success and unexpected setbacks.

Start-Up Costs

Start-up cost breakdown—A pie chart showing the percentage of budget allocated to key categories like land acquisition, construction, furnishings, permits, and marketing.

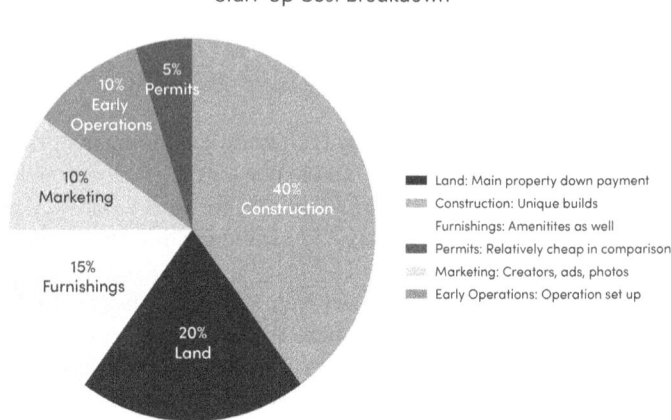

There is no *Shark Tank* for people looking to start a glamping business unfortunately (does anyone have a direct line to Mark Cuban?). When I first started my financial planning, I had a set amount to spend, and I had to make some real-world sacrifices to get it. I had around $30,000 saved to spend and also took out a home equity line of credit on my primary residence of around $75,000. I knew it was going to take some up-front capital to get my business and investment started. Start-up costs are the initial investments required to launch your hospitality business. These costs can vary dramatically depending on the size, location, and nature of your operation. For a glamping site or short-term rental, start-up costs might include land acquisition or lease expenses, construction and renovation costs, furnishings, permits, licenses, and initial marketing expenditures.

- **Property acquisition or leasing:** The cost of acquiring land or leasing a property is typically one of the largest initial investments. This category might include deposit fees, legal costs, appraisal fees, and any necessary renovations to make the space suitable for hospitality purposes.

- **Construction and renovation:** If you are building or renovating a property to transform it into a glamping site or rental space, construction costs are a significant component. These costs include building materials, labor, permits, and contingency funds for unexpected expenses.
- **Furnishings and equipment:** Creating a memorable guest experience often requires high-quality furnishings, decor, and equipment. Think of comfortable beds, stylish furniture, kitchen appliances, outdoor seating, and technological amenities like smart locks or automated check-in systems.
- **Licensing, permits, and insurance:** Regulatory compliance is nonnegotiable. Start-up costs must account for obtaining the necessary licenses and permits, as well as securing insurance to protect your property and business operations. Costs can include business licenses, health and safety certifications, and liability insurance.
- **Initial marketing and branding:** Launching a new hospitality venture requires an effective marketing campaign to generate early interest and bookings. Initial expenditures might include website development, branding, social media promotions, and partnerships with local tourism boards.

I remember spending countless hours researching what it would cost to build my first geo dome, as I talked about at the beginning of the chapter. I talked to people who had built one, picked the brains of contractors and vendors, and reached out to anyone with the word "geo" in their bio—I may have even messaged a few geography teachers by mistake.

Despite all that planning, I still went about 50 percent over budget on my first build. That same $60,000 I thought I would spend ballooned to almost $90,000 by the time I was done. But the experience was invaluable. Luckily, I started small, and any mistake I made wasn't compounded by having a massive 1,000-square-foot build. Mine was only 426 square feet, and I knew that I would be more prepared to tackle the bigger sizes after. I learned more from that one project than any forum thread or YouTube video could've taught me. Sometimes, the best lessons come from building—and adjusting—in real time.

Creating a detailed start-up cost estimate is the first step in effective financial planning. Many entrepreneurs find it useful to create a spreadsheet that itemizes every potential expense. Experts recommend adding a contingency budget of 10–20 percent on top of your projected start-up costs to accommodate unforeseen expenses. I may not be a financial or construction expert, but I can almost guarantee you will hit that 20 percent mark—and that's if you are lucky. I don't say this to intimidate you but more to bring clarity on what exactly to expect.

Once you have a clear picture of your start-up costs, the next step is to determine how you will finance your venture. Financing options include personal savings, loans from financial institutions, angel investors, venture capital, or even crowdfunding platforms. Each financing option has its own set of advantages and trade-offs. For instance, while personal savings can reduce the need for debt, they may also limit your ability to invest in growth. On the other hand, loans can provide necessary capital but add a recurring repayment burden to your operating expenses.

Operating Budgets

Operating Budget for Glamping Operators			
Category	Description	Estimated Range	Notes / Tips
Property Managment	Software, admin help, or VA fees	$100–$500	Use tools like Hospitable or Lodgify
Utilities	Water, electric, propane, solar maintenance	$150–$600	Off-grid may lower or shift costs
Internet & Tech	Wi-Fi, smart lock systems, security cams	$50–$200	Starlink can work in rural areas
Cleaning & Laundry	Per-turn cleaning, linen service, supplies	$200–$600+	Higher in peak season or with frequent turnover
Maintenance & Repairs	General fixes, seasonal upkeep	$100–$400	Budget more for remote/rural properties
Insurance	STR-specific policy (liability + property)	$100–$300	STR insurance is separate from standard homeowners
Trash & Septic	Waste service or dumps, septic pumping	$50–$250	Especially important for off-grid setups

Category	Description	Estimated Range	Notes / Tips
Supplies & Restocking	TP, paper towels, soaps, snacks, wood, etc.	$75–$250	Track usage and set up monthly inventory checks
Marketing & Advertising	Paid ads, SEO, influencer outreach	$100–$400	Ramp this up for new listings or off-season boosts
Taxes & Fees	Local STR tax, lodging tax, platform fees (Airbnb/Vrbo)	10%–15% of revenue	Keep separate for quarterly filing or escrow account
Miscellaneous	Contingency for surprises	$50–$150	Always have wiggle room

After over three years of running my site, I can easily say managing your operating expenses is only second to the amount of revenue you can bring in. They work hand in hand to reach the cash flow and business value you desire. I remember the first time I got my insurance quote back for commercial liability insurance on my property, and I almost fainted. I had budgeted only $250 a month, and with all of my insurance costs, it ended up being closer to $800 for all units. I learned quickly that for any next project, I needed to get estimates before and work on what exactly I would spend in my operating budget yearly.

An operating budget is a detailed projection of your expected revenue and expenses over a specific period, usually on a monthly, quarterly, or annual basis. It serves as a road map for managing your day-to-day operations and ensures that you are allocating resources efficiently. Operating budgets help you monitor performance, identify potential cash flow issues early, and make informed decisions about where to cut costs or invest in growth.

- **Revenue projections:** Begin by forecasting your expected revenue from bookings, additional services, and ancillary income. This can include seasonal variations, occupancy rates, ADRs, and revenue per available rental (RevPAR).
- **Fixed expenses:** These are expenses that remain constant regardless of your occupancy levels, such as property leases, mortgage payments, insurance premiums, and salaries for full-time staff.
- **Variable expenses:** Variable expenses fluctuate based on business activity. For a hospitality business, these might

include utilities, maintenance, cleaning services, marketing costs, and commission fees for third-party booking platforms.
- **Capital expenditures (CapEx):** Although typically planned for separately from operating expenses, capital expenditures—such as major renovations or the purchase of long-term assets—should be factored into your overall financial planning.
- **Contingency funds:** Building a buffer into your operating budget is crucial. A contingency fund covers unexpected costs such as emergency repairs, unanticipated regulatory fees, or sudden drops in occupancy.

Developing an operating budget involves historical data analysis (if available), market research, and realistic forecasting. For new ventures, benchmarking against similar businesses can be invaluable. Tools such as QuickBooks, FreshBooks, or specialized hospitality budgeting software can simplify the process. It also sometimes just takes starting small, so you can understand how your business will operate in your specific area. I never realized that my landscaping budget would need to be so high, as grass in Texas grows faster than I can blink. I needed some real-world experience to eventually figure out what my target spend was for certain categories.

Regularly reviewing your operating budget is critical to understanding it. Many successful property managers set up monthly or quarterly reviews to compare actual expenses and revenues against their projections. This process allows you to identify trends, adjust your spending, and implement cost-saving measures before small issues become significant financial burdens.

Operating budgets are not set in stone. As market conditions change—due to seasonality, economic shifts, or unexpected events—it's essential to revisit and adjust your budget. A flexible budget allows you to respond to challenges and opportunities in real time, ensuring that your business remains financially agile and sustainable.

Revenue Forecasting

Projecting your budget, especially when new, is more difficult than I ever anticipated. AirDNA was telling me I would make $25,000 a year and "gurus" on the internet were telling me I'd make $500,000 a year (kidding but not really). I struggled with my fair share of budgets through college (my Whataburger budget should not have existed). How can you even begin to predict the future of your revenue? Data, technology, and some creative sleuthing on competitors.

Revenue forecasting is the process of estimating future income based on historical data, market trends, and various influencing factors, such as occupancy rates, ADR, and seasonal demand. In the hospitality industry, accurate revenue forecasting is critical, as it informs budgeting, staffing, marketing strategies, and overall business planning.

- **Historical data analysis.** If you have been operating for a while, your past performance is one of the best indicators of future revenue. Analyzing trends in occupancy, ADR, and RevPAR can help you project future performance with reasonable accuracy.
- **Market analysis.** Understanding the local market, competition, and industry trends is key to accurate forecasting. For example, if a major event is scheduled in your area, you might anticipate a surge in bookings that could positively impact your revenue.
- **Seasonal adjustments.** The hospitality industry is highly seasonal. Use historical seasonal data to adjust your revenue forecasts. Many forecasting tools allow you to input seasonal variations so that your projections reflect the realities of peak and off-peak periods.
- **Scenario planning.** Create multiple revenue scenarios—optimistic, realistic, and pessimistic—to prepare for different market conditions. This approach helps you build flexibility into your financial planning and ensures that you are prepared for unexpected downturns or booms.

Modern technology has greatly simplified revenue forecasting. Software tools such as Beyond Pricing, PriceLabs, and specialized property management systems can automate much of the forecasting process. These tools use real-time data and advanced algorithms to predict future revenue, often integrating with your dynamic pricing strategies to provide a cohesive financial management system.

Say you're looking at your numbers for the next quarter and they look a little soft—maybe fewer bookings than usual or a big gap in

February. Instead of panicking, you can make a plan. Maybe you hold off on that new outdoor swing set you were about to install, or you double down on Facebook ads targeting spring break travelers. Some glamping owners even run flash sales or create new themed packages ("February Firepit & Wine Weekend") to fill in those slower periods.

The best part? When you make forecasting part of your regular rhythm—whether it's monthly or quarterly—you stop making decisions based on vibes and start making them based on facts. That means your staffing stays lean during quiet seasons, your maintenance projects don't eat into busy weekends, and you're investing in the right things at the right time. Even something as simple as using a shared Google Sheet with projected revenue, expenses, and actual results can completely change how confident you feel running your business. It's not about perfection—it's about staying one step ahead of the game.

Cash Flow Management

Let's be honest: If you are reading this book, you are interested in the cash flow that can be earned with glamping sites. What you do with your cash flow is critical in making sure it will be there for years to come. Cash flow management is important for any business, especially in the hospitality industry, where revenue can be highly seasonal and expenses are often fixed. Maintaining a positive cash flow ensures that you have the liquidity to cover daily operating expenses, reinvest in your property, and navigate unexpected financial challenges.

- **Receivables and collections.** Ensure that payments from bookings and other sources are collected in a timely manner. Delays in receiving funds can disrupt your cash flow, even if your revenue figures look healthy on paper.
- **Payables management.** Monitor your expenses carefully. Prioritize payments for essential services and negotiate favorable terms with suppliers where possible. Keeping a tight rein on payables helps maintain a steady cash flow and avoid unnecessary shortfalls.
- **Cash reserves.** A healthy business always maintains a cash reserve. These reserves can be used to cover unexpected expenses, such as emergency repairs or a sudden drop in occupancy. Experts typically recommend setting aside at least three to six months' worth of operating expenses.

- **Forecasting cash flow.** Just as with revenue forecasting, cash flow forecasting is essential. By predicting when cash inflows and outflows will occur, you can anticipate potential shortfalls and plan accordingly. Many property management systems offer cash flow forecasting tools that integrate with your revenue and expense data.

Improving cash flow in your glamping business doesn't mean pinching every penny—it means getting smart about how money moves in and out of your operation. Start by tightening up your operations. That could mean switching to energy-efficient systems, automating parts of your guest communication, or renegotiating with vendors who are quietly overcharging you just because they can.

Don't be afraid to ask for flexible payment terms from your suppliers. If you can spread out big expenses during slow seasons, your bank account will thank you. And while you're at it, keep a close eye on your cash flow statements. A quick weekly or monthly review can help you catch issues early—before they snowball into full-on budget emergencies.

You can also nudge guests to help your cash flow along by offering small perks for early payments or extended stays. It creates more predictable revenue and cuts down on those last-minute "something came up" cancellations. When cash is king, creativity is your best currency.

Modern financial management software can automate many aspects of cash flow management. Tools like QuickBooks, Xero, and specialized hospitality management platforms offer real-time insights into your cash flow, helping you make data-driven decisions. By integrating these tools into your overall financial planning, you can ensure that your business maintains healthy liquidity even in volatile market conditions.

Best Practices for Long-Term Financial Health

- **Regular financial reviews.** Conduct regular financial reviews—monthly, quarterly, and annually—to compare actual performance against your projections. This practice helps you identify trends, adjust strategies, and ensure that your financial planning remains aligned with your business goals.

- **Maintain a strong cash reserve.** Prioritize building and maintaining a healthy cash reserve. A robust reserve can cushion your business against unexpected expenses or downturns, ensuring continuity even in challenging times.
- **Continually update your forecasts.** The hospitality industry is dynamic, and market conditions can change rapidly. Update your revenue forecasts and operating budgets frequently to reflect the latest trends, ensuring that your planning remains relevant and effective.
- **Invest in professional advice.** Engage with financial advisors, accountants, and industry consultants who can offer insights specific to the hospitality market. Their expertise can help you navigate complex financial decisions and optimize your strategy.
- **Monitor key performance indicators (KPIs).** Track KPIs such as occupancy rates, ADR, RevPAR, and cash flow ratios. These metrics provide a snapshot of your financial health and can guide strategic adjustments.

Final Thoughts

Financial planning isn't a box you check once—it's a living, breathing part of your business that requires constant attention, strategic thinking, and the ability to adapt. From understanding your start-up costs and building detailed operating budgets to accurately forecasting revenue and managing cash flow, every step helps create a financial foundation built for long-term success.

Every dollar you spend—from launch day to daily operations—plays a role in your growth. A strong financial plan doesn't just help you survive the ups and downs; it positions you to seize new opportunities with confidence. By using smart tools, sticking to proven best practices, and staying flexible, you'll gain the clarity needed to grow your business while maintaining control over your bottom line.

Just as you invest in your property and guest experience, you need to invest in your financial strategy. The ability to adapt to market shifts, manage expenses, and secure funding for future growth is what separates short-lived ventures from lasting ones. With the right systems in place, you're not just building a business—you're building a profitable, scalable brand that's ready for whatever comes next.

As you put the strategies from this chapter into action, remember financial planning is a journey, not a destination. Stay curious, keep refining your approach, and use your numbers as a tool—not a hurdle. In a fast-moving industry where margins matter, a well-executed financial plan isn't just helpful—it's your greatest competitive advantage.

Lessons from the Field

- **Know your start-up costs.** Budget for land, construction, furnishings, permits, and marketing.
- **Create an operating budget.** Track revenue, fixed/variable expenses, and contingency funds.
- **Forecast revenue accurately.** Use historical data, market trends, and seasonal adjustments.
- **Manage cash flow.** Maintain reserves, streamline expenses, and monitor payables/receivables.
- **Explore financing options.** Consider loans, investors, crowdfunding, or alternative funding.
- **Use technology for financial planning.** Leverage budgeting, forecasting, and cash flow tools.

Chapter 15

Performance Metrics

Running a successful glamping business requires more than just a beautifully designed tent or cabin in a scenic location. To truly optimize performance, you need to measure and analyze key performance indicators (KPIs) that directly impact your revenue, profitability, and long-term sustainability. In this chapter, we'll explore the most critical performance metrics for a glamping business, how to track them, and strategies to improve your results.

Key Performance Indicators (KPIs) for Glamping Businesses

Key performance indicators (KPIs) are measurable values that indicate how well your glamping site is performing. By regularly tracking these metrics, you can identify strengths, weaknesses, and opportunities for growth.

Here are the most essential KPIs for a glamping operation.

- **Occupancy rate:** The percentage of nights your glamping units are booked compared to the total available nights.
- **Average daily rate (ADR):** The average revenue earned per occupied unit per night.
- **Revenue per available room (RevPAR):** A measure of revenue earned per available unit, accounting for both occupancy and pricing.
- **Guest acquisition cost (GAC):** The amount spent on marketing and advertising to acquire a single booking.
- **Cost per stay:** The total cost of servicing a guest per stay, including cleaning, maintenance, and amenities.
- **Profit margin:** The percentage of total revenue that remains after expenses.
- **Length of Stay (LOS):** The average number of nights per booking.
- **Direct booking rate:** The percentage of reservations made directly through your website or other non-OTA (online travel agency) channels.

- **Guest satisfaction score:** A measure of guest experience based on reviews and feedback.

By tracking these KPIs, you can make data-driven decisions that improve efficiency and profitability.

KPI Formulas	
Occupancy rate	= (Occupied nights ÷ total available nights) × 100
Average daily rate (ADR)	= Total revenue ÷ number of occupied nights
Revenue per available room (RevPAR)	= Occupancy rate × ADR
Guest acquisition cost (GAC)	= Total marketing spend ÷ number of bookings
Cost per stay	= (Cleaning + maintenance + amenities) ÷ total stays
Profit margin	= [(Total revenue − total expenses) ÷ total revenue] × 100
Length of Stay (LOS)	= Total nights booked ÷ total bookings
Direct booking rate	= (Direct bookings ÷ total bookings) × 100
Guest satisfaction score	= (Total review score ÷ number of reviews) × 100

Occupancy Rates: The Key Glamping Revenue Driver

Occupancy rate is one of the most important metrics for any short-term rental business, including glamping. It is calculated using the following formula:

$$\text{Occupancy rate (\%)} = \frac{\text{Total Nights Booked}}{\text{Total Nights Available}} \times 100$$

For example, if you have five glamping units available for thirty days in a month (150 total available nights) and 120 nights were booked, your occupancy rate would be:

$$\frac{120}{150} \times 100 = 80\%$$

Several factors can impact your occupancy rate, including:

- **Seasonality:** Peak travel seasons will naturally have higher occupancy, while slow seasons may require special pricing strategies.
- **Marketing efforts:** A strong online presence, social media marketing, and partnerships with travel influencers can help attract guests.
- **Competitive pricing:** Your pricing strategy should reflect demand and competition while maintaining profitability.
- **Guest experience and reviews:** Positive reviews boost credibility and increase future bookings.
- **Booking channels:** Listing on multiple platforms (Airbnb, Vrbo, direct website) increases visibility.

Boosting occupancy takes a combination of creativity, timing, and understanding your audience. Offering seasonal discounts or limited-time promotions during off-peak months can help keep bookings steady year-round. At the same time, implementing smart minimum stay policies ensures you're maximizing revenue from each reservation without leaving unnecessary gaps in your calendar.

Email marketing is another powerful tool—reaching out to past guests with exclusive offers or personalized messages can turn one-time visitors into loyal fans. And don't underestimate the draw of curated experiences. Promoting themed getaways like wellness retreats, adventure weekends, or romantic escapes can help you tap into niche markets and give travelers a reason to book *your* stay over anyone else's.

Average Daily Rate (ADR): Setting the Right Price

ADR measures the average revenue earned per occupied night. It is calculated as:

$$\text{ADR} = \frac{\text{Total Revenue}}{\text{Number of Nights Booked}}$$

For example, if your glamping site earns $12,000 from 100 booked nights, your ADR would be:

$$\frac{\$12,000}{100} = \$120 \text{ per night}$$

While a high ADR is desirable, setting rates too high can reduce occupancy. Here's how to optimize ADR:

- **Use dynamic pricing.** Adjust rates based on demand, seasonality, and local events.
- **Offer upsells and add-ons.** Enhance the guest experience with premium services like private dining, guided tours, or spa packages.
- **Leverage reviews and Superhost status.** Higher-rated listings can justify premium pricing.
- **Analyze competitor pricing.** Stay competitive by benchmarking against similar glamping sites in your area.

By balancing ADR with occupancy rates, you can maximize overall revenue.

Revenue Per Available Room (RevPAR): Measuring Revenue Efficiency

RevPAR is a key metric that combines occupancy and ADR to give a complete picture of revenue efficiency. It is calculated as:

$$\text{RevPAR} = \text{ADR} \times \text{Occupancy Rate}$$

For example, if your ADR is $150 and your occupancy rate is 70 percent, your RevPAR would be:

$$\$150 \times 70\% = \$105$$

RevPAR helps determine if your pricing and occupancy strategies are working effectively. A low RevPAR may indicate that your rates are too low or that occupancy is not optimized.

- **Bundle experiences:** Offer multi-night discounts with added experiences like local excursions.
- **Optimize booking windows:** Encourage early bookings with discounts while keeping last-minute pricing competitive.
- **Improve guest experience:** Happy guests leave great reviews, leading to higher occupancy and pricing power.

Cost Control Measures

Running a successful glamping business isn't just about offering a beautiful escape—it's also about managing costs effectively to maximize profits. By implementing smart strategies in key areas like cleaning, maintenance, utilities, and marketing, you can keep expenses low without compromising the guest experience.

Maintaining a pristine environment is essential for guest satisfaction, but it can quickly become one of your biggest expenses. One way to cut costs over time is by using eco-friendly cleaning products. Not only are they better for the environment, but they often require less product per use and reduce wear and tear on surfaces. Additionally, preventive maintenance is key to avoiding expensive emergency repairs. Regularly checking for leaks, weatherproofing structures, and servicing HVAC systems can prevent major issues from arising.

Automating check-in and checkout processes is another way to cut labor costs. Implementing keyless entry, automated guest communication, and digital guidebooks allows guests to navigate their stay independently while reducing the need for on-site staff. This not only saves money but also enhances the guest experience by providing seamless, contactless service.

Energy and water usage can add up quickly in a glamping business, especially if guests aren't mindful of their consumption. Investing in solar panels or energy-efficient appliances can significantly cut long-term expenses by reducing dependency on traditional utilities. While the up-front cost may be higher, the long-term savings often justify the investment.

Encouraging guests to conserve water and electricity is another simple but effective strategy. Small actions like installing low-flow showerheads, using motion-sensor lighting, and providing gentle reminders through signage can make a big difference. Some hosts even incentivize conservation efforts by offering discounts or small rewards to guests who help minimize their environmental impact.

The cost of restocking supplies and replacing furnishings can quickly add up, but strategic purchasing can help keep expenses in check. Buying essentials like toiletries, cleaning supplies, and linens in bulk can lead to significant savings over time. Look for wholesale suppliers or bulk purchase programs designed for hospitality businesses to maximize discounts.

When it comes to furnishings, it's important to balance quality with durability. Opting for high-quality yet durable materials means fewer replacements in the long run. Instead of choosing trendy but flimsy furniture, invest in pieces designed for heavy use. This not only reduces replacement costs but also ensures that your glamping site maintains a polished, well-maintained look for years to come.

One of the biggest drains on profitability in the short-term rental industry is the reliance on online travel agencies (OTAs) like Airbnb and Vrbo. While these platforms are great for visibility, their commission fees can eat into profits. To reduce dependence on OTAs, focus on increasing direct bookings through social media, SEO, and an engaging website. A well-optimized website with an easy-to-use booking system allows guests to book directly, eliminating third-party fees.

Loyalty programs and referral discounts are another powerful way to encourage repeat customers and word-of-mouth marketing. Offering a small discount for returning guests or rewarding guests who refer friends can create a steady stream of bookings without the need for paid advertising. Since glamping often attracts adventure seekers and nature lovers who enjoy sharing their experiences, these strategies can be especially effective in building a loyal customer base.

By implementing these cost-saving measures, you can keep your glamping business running efficiently while maximizing profits. Thoughtful investments in maintenance, energy efficiency, smart purchasing, and direct marketing will pay off in the long run, ensuring your business remains financially sustainable while offering an exceptional guest experience.

Calculating Profit Margins

Profitability is the ultimate goal of any glamping business. To calculate your profit margin, use the following formula:

$$\text{Profit Margin (\%)} = \frac{\text{Total Revenue} - \text{Total Expenses}}{\text{Total Revenue}} \times 100$$

For example, if your glamping site earns $50,000 in revenue and expenses total $35,000, your profit margin is:

$$\frac{\$50{,}000 - \$35{,}000}{\$50{,}000} \times 100 = 30\%$$

Analyzing Performance Trends

Regularly reviewing your KPIs will reveal trends that help improve profitability. For example:

- If occupancy is high but ADR is low, you may need to increase pricing.
- If expenses are rising, look for cost-cutting opportunities without hurting guest satisfaction.

Long-Term Strategies for Profit Growth

- Expand with additional units or unique accommodations like tree houses or domes.
- Introduce recurring revenue streams like memberships, retreats, or glamping gear rentals.
- Diversify marketing efforts with partnerships and local collaborations.

Performance metrics are essential for any successful glamping business. By regularly tracking and optimizing KPIs, like occupancy rates, ADR, and RevPAR, you can maximize revenue while maintaining efficiency. Cost-control measures and profitability analysis ensure your business remains sustainable and scalable in the long run.

Taking the time to analyze these metrics not only helps improve daily operations but also positions your glamping site for long-term growth and success. Whether you're just starting or looking to scale, performance tracking is the key to unlocking higher profits and an exceptional guest experience.

Final Thoughts

Running a glamping business might start with a vision—beautiful spaces, memorable guest experiences, and the freedom of creative entrepreneurship—but it's sustained by the numbers. Performance metrics like occupancy rate, ADR, RevPAR, and guest acquisition cost aren't just technical jargon—they're the dashboard for your business. They help you make confident decisions, adjust in real time, and avoid costly guesswork. Without tracking them, it's like trying to drive cross-country without a map.

As you grow your glamping site, you'll face both operational challenges and incredible opportunities. The key is to build a foundation based on measurable performance and consistent analysis. Knowing how much you spend to acquire each guest, how efficiently your space is monetized, and what your true profit margins are will allow you to reinvest wisely—whether that means adding new amenities, hiring help, or expanding to new locations.

In the end, the magic of glamping is in the experience—but the sustainability is in the systems. Combining creative hospitality with data-driven performance ensures your business doesn't just survive—it thrives. The best hosts aren't just dreamers—they're also dialed in operators. And now, with the right tools, formulas, and focus, you're one step closer to becoming both.

Lessons from the Field

- **Track key KPIs.** Monitor occupancy, ADR, RevPAR, guest acquisition costs, and profit margins.
- **Optimize occupancy rates.** Use seasonal discounts, minimum stays, and direct booking strategies.
- **Maximize ADR and RevPAR.** Implement dynamic pricing, upsell experiences, and analyze competitor rates.
- **Control costs.** Reduce expenses in cleaning, utilities, supplies, and OTA fees without sacrificing quality.

- **Analyze profitability.** Regularly review revenue vs. expenses to adjust pricing and improve efficiency.
- **Scale for growth.** Expand unique accommodations, introduce memberships, and diversify marketing efforts.

Part 6
Growth and Innovation

Chapter 16

Scaling Your Business

If you're serious about building a real business, scaling is where things get exciting. I used to think one glamping site was enough—until I realized how much knowledge and experience I'd gained. Suddenly, I wasn't just running a site—I was building something valuable. With each new location, your costs go down, your systems get sharper, your revenue grows, and you actually free up more of your time—if you scale the right way.

Growing a glamping business isn't just about adding more units— it's about building smarter. Whether you're expanding your current site, opening new ones, exploring franchises, or forming key partnerships, the right strategy will help you grow while keeping your brand experience strong and your business sustainable.

In this chapter, we'll explore different expansion strategies, the challenges of managing multiple locations, the potential of franchising, the benefits of partnerships, and how to innovate in guest experience to set your brand apart in the increasingly competitive glamping market.

Scaling Strategies Comparison					
Scaling Strategy	Investment Required	Operational Complexity	Time to Scale	Risk Level	Revenue Potential
Expand to New Locations	High	High	Slow	High	High
Increase Units at Existing Site	Medium	Moderate	Fast	Low	Moderate to High
Franchising	Low to Medium	High	Slow	High	High (if successful)
Partnerships & Joint Ventures	Medium	Moderate	Moderate	Medium	High

Expansion Strategies: Growing Beyond One Location

When scaling a glamping business, expansion should be strategic rather than reactive. Consider where, how, and when to grow while maintaining profitability and quality.

Before opening a second site, ensuring your current location is operating at its highest revenue potential is the smartest financial move.

Expanding too quickly without fully optimizing your existing property can leave money on the table and create unnecessary financial strain. Instead of rushing into a new location, consider ways to maximize your current site's profitability by increasing occupancy, enhancing guest experiences, and diversifying income streams.

One of the most effective ways to grow revenue is by adding more accommodations, if demand supports it. If your site consistently books out, introducing additional tents, domes, cabins, or tree houses allows you to capitalize on that interest without the need for extensive new marketing efforts. Since your brand is already established and attracting guests, expanding capacity is often a natural step toward higher profitability.

Beyond increasing the number of units, enhancing guest amenities can significantly boost revenue per stay. High-value features such as hot tubs, private firepits, outdoor dining experiences, or guided excursions add to the overall appeal of a glamping site. Guests are often willing to pay a premium for luxury elements that elevate their stay, creating opportunities for upselling. For example, offering a private stargazing experience with a telescope and blankets or a chef-prepared meal delivered to their tent can enhance both guest satisfaction and your bottom line.

Another powerful way to increase revenue is by hosting events and retreats. Glamping sites are perfect for intimate weddings, corporate team-building retreats, wellness getaways, and even creative workshops. By marketing your property as an event-friendly destination, you can tap into new customer segments and generate higher earnings from group bookings. These events often come with additional revenue opportunities through catering, guided activities, and premium lodging packages.

Seasonal experiences can also play a major role in extending profitability beyond peak travel months. Many glamping businesses thrive during warmer months, but adding winter-friendly accommodations such as heated domes or insulated cabins can open up new revenue opportunities. Holiday-themed stays, such as Christmas tree farm experiences, cozy winter retreats with mulled wine and firepits, or fall foliage getaways with pumpkin-carving workshops, create unique offerings that attract guests year-round. Adjusting your marketing to highlight these seasonal packages can help drive demand even when traditional glamping seasons slow down.

Maximizing revenue from your existing location before expanding ensures a strong financial foundation and a more sustainable growth strategy. By increasing capacity, enhancing the guest experience, leveraging event hosting, and tapping into seasonal demand, you can build a thriving business that is not only profitable but also well-prepared for future expansion.

Expanding to a New Location

Once your first glamping site is running efficiently and generating consistent revenue, you're likely going to start thinking about expansion. Opening a second location can increase profitability and brand recognition, but it requires careful planning to ensure success. Choosing the right market is crucial, and this begins with analyzing short-term rental demand. Platforms like AirDNA can provide insights into occupancy rates, average daily rates, and seasonality trends in potential locations. Understanding demand helps you avoid oversaturated areas and instead focus on destinations with high traveler interest but limited competition. You don't want to just expand but thrive in your new location.

Proximity to tourist attractions is another key factor. Locations near national parks, beaches, hiking trails, or wineries naturally attract visitors seeking outdoor experiences. These destinations often have a built-in demand for glamping stays, making them ideal for expansion. You can take all of your experience from your first site and eliminate the mistakes you made the first time. Accessibility also plays a major role in site selection. Even the most stunning location can struggle if guests have difficulty getting there. Ensuring reliable roads, available utilities, and a strong supply chain for maintenance and housekeeping is essential.

Regulatory compliance should never be overlooked in new locations. Different regions have varying zoning laws, short-term rental restrictions, and environmental regulations that could impact your ability to operate. Before committing to a new location, research local policies thoroughly to avoid costly legal challenges down the road. Consulting with a local real estate attorney or planning expert can help streamline the process and ensure your new site is fully compliant.

Beyond expanding to a new location, diversifying the types of accommodations you offer can attract a wider range of guests. Luxury tree houses, for example, are highly sought after by high-end travelers looking for unique and photogenic stays. These structures often command premium rates due to their exclusivity and immersive nature experience. A-frame cabins, on the other hand, offer a trendy yet cozy retreat that balances rustic charm with modern comfort, making them appealing to a broad audience.

For travelers focused on sustainability, eco-pods and off-grid units provide an attractive option. These accommodations cater to guests who prioritize environmental consciousness and self-sufficiency, making them perfect for destinations that promote sustainable tourism. Similarly, floating cabins or houseboats present a unique opportunity for glamping businesses located near lakes, rivers, or coastal regions. The novelty of staying on the water can differentiate your site from competitors and create an unforgettable guest experience.

Another growing trend is the inclusion of RV and camper van sites. Digital nomads and road trippers are a niche yet expanding market that values well-equipped camping spots with access to Wi-Fi, power hookups, and communal amenities. Providing dedicated spaces for this segment can create an additional revenue stream while increasing occupancy rates during slower seasons.

Expanding a glamping business requires more than just replicating what worked in the first location. It's about strategically selecting new markets, ensuring operational efficiency, and offering diverse accommodations that appeal to different traveler preferences. Whether scaling to a second site or simply adding new types of units, thoughtful expansion can drive long-term success and establish your brand as a leader in the glamping industry.

Multiple Location Management

Expanding to multiple locations introduces new operational challenges. Managing logistics, maintaining consistent guest experiences, and ensuring efficient resource allocation become critical.

- **Create an operational playbook.** Document everything from guest check-in procedures to cleaning protocols so new locations run seamlessly.
- **Implement property management systems (PMS).** Use platforms like Hospitable to centralize booking management, pricing, and guest communication.
- **Develop a remote monitoring system.** Use smart locks, security cameras, and remote thermostat controls to streamline operations.

- **Train local staff or hire property managers.** Establish a strong, on-site team that aligns with your brand's service standards.

Managing multiple locations requires a strong digital infrastructure. Consider:

- **Cloud-based booking and payment systems.** Allow guests to book seamlessly across multiple locations.
- **Automated guest communication.** Use AI chatbots and automated messages to handle FAQs, check-in instructions, and post-stay follow-ups.
- **Remote maintenance tracking.** Smart sensors can detect leaks, power outages, and HVAC issues, preventing costly repairs.

To scale successfully, it's important to focus on systems—not just adding more locations. Regular site visits or audits help ensure brand consistency across all properties, while mystery guest programs can provide unbiased insights into the guest experience. Guest feedback surveys are another valuable tool to continuously refine and improve services. By standardizing processes and automating wherever possible, you can avoid mismanagement, keep guests happy, and maintain the quality that made your first site successful in the first place.

Franchise Opportunities

You may hear the word *franchising* and think of something like McDonald's or Starbucks. A lot of the most successful companies in this space have expanded rapidly and beyond their wildest dreams by simply using this type of model. Before considering franchising, it's important to evaluate whether your glamping business is truly ready for expansion under a franchise model. A strong and recognizable brand is the foundation of a successful franchise. If your business has a distinct identity, a compelling unique selling proposition (USP), and a loyal customer base, it becomes more attractive to potential franchisees who want to align with an already successful concept. A glamping brand that stands out—whether through unique accommodations, exceptional guest experiences, or a strong social media presence—has a far greater chance of attracting quality franchise partners.

Beyond branding, the business model itself must be tested and proven to be consistently profitable. A location that generates high occupancy, maintains strong reviews, and operates efficiently is a sign that the model can be replicated. Franchisees will only be interested if they see a clear path to success, so demonstrating profitability and a solid return on investment is crucial. Along with a strong business model, offering franchisees comprehensive support is key. This includes training programs, marketing assistance, operational playbooks, and standardized booking systems that make it easier for new owners to succeed. Without these resources, franchisees may struggle to maintain the brand's reputation and guest experience standards, ultimately impacting the entire franchise network.

Scalability is another major factor in determining franchise readiness. If the business relies heavily on custom-built structures, hyperlocal supplier relationships, or unique guest experiences that are difficult to replicate, expansion can become complicated. Instead, standardizing designs, securing bulk supplier agreements, and implementing streamlined booking and operational systems creates a model that can be efficiently duplicated in multiple locations. The more seamless the replication process, the more appealing the franchise opportunity becomes.

When structuring the franchise model, there are multiple approaches to consider. A full franchise model provides a turnkey glamping business where franchisees pay an up-front fee and ongoing royalties in exchange for a complete operational blueprint, brand recognition, and ongoing support. This approach is ideal for those who want a fully structured business model with minimal guesswork. A hybrid model allows franchisees to operate under the brand while maintaining control over pricing and day-to-day management. This offers more flexibility but requires strong brand guidelines to maintain consistency. Alternatively, a licensing agreement enables property owners to use the brand name and marketing power while operating independently, making it a lower-commitment option with fewer ongoing obligations for both parties.

The benefits of franchising extend beyond rapid expansion. Since franchisees invest their own capital into launching new locations, the financial burden on the original owner is significantly reduced. This allows for faster scaling without requiring massive up-front investments. Additionally, franchisees contribute to brand-wide marketing efforts, creating a shared promotional strategy that benefits all locations. As more locations open, brand awareness naturally increases, enhancing credibility and making it easier to attract both guests and new franchisees.

By building a well-structured, replicable business model, glamping entrepreneurs can expand nationally or even globally with minimal direct capital investment. Franchising offers a way to scale while maintaining brand integrity and leveraging the motivation of independent operators who are invested in the success of their own locations. When done right, it creates a win-win scenario where the original owner grows their brand, franchisees enter a proven business model, and guests continue to experience high-quality stays across multiple destinations.

Partnership Development: Collaborating for Growth

Strategic partnerships are one of the fastest ways to grow your glamping business while keeping costs low. You don't have to do it all alone—especially when there are landowners and local businesses that would love to collaborate.

For example, some rural landowners have beautiful properties but no clue how to run a glamping operation. That's where you come in. Partnering with them lets you expand your brand without having to buy more land. Everyone wins. You can also work with local businesses to elevate the guest experience. Bring in a food truck on weekends, collaborate with a local chef for curated dinners, or connect with tour operators to offer things like wine tastings, horseback rides, or kayak trips. Partnering with wellness providers to host yoga retreats or meditation workshops can also add a whole new layer of value for your guests.

And if you want to stand out as a sustainable brand, team up with eco-focused organizations. Think tree-planting initiatives, carbon offset programs, or waste management solutions that help you walk the talk on sustainability. At the end of the day, scaling isn't just about more units—it's about offering better experiences. Guests come back (and bring their friends) when you deliver something memorable.

Think: themed cabins with immersive storytelling, like a 1920s speakeasy or a sci-fi pod. Add a scavenger hunt, a nature guide, or a personalized welcome basket with local wine and snacks—you're not just hosting a stay, you're creating a story people want to share. The glamping brands that win aren't just the biggest—they're the most thoughtful, the most creative, and the ones who know how to use partnerships to their advantage.

Final Thoughts

Scaling a glamping business is an exciting journey that requires thoughtful planning, strong operational systems, and innovative guest experiences. Whether you expand through new locations, franchising, or partnerships, success lies in maintaining quality, managing efficiently, and continually innovating to offer unique, memorable stays.

By leveraging technology, sustainability, and high-touch hospitality, your glamping brand can grow profitably, sustainably, and in alignment with modern traveler expectations.

Lessons from the Field

- **Expand strategically.** Maximize revenue at your current site before opening new locations.
- **Standardize operations.** Use SOPs, property management systems, and automation for consistency.
- **Franchise for faster growth.** A proven model, strong branding, and franchisee support are key.
- **Leverage partnerships.** Work with landowners, local businesses, and ecotourism initiatives.
- **Innovate guest experiences.** Personalization, themed stays, and unique amenities drive bookings.
- **Prioritize sustainability.** Off-grid features, solar power, and eco-conscious designs attract modern travelers.

Chapter 17

Future Trends in Glamping

I'm not a fortune teller—if I were, I might've just retired by correctly guessing which crypto coin to buy in 2014 or predicting how many towels guests really use per weekend. But what I can tell you is this: The future of glamping is incredibly exciting.

The industry is changing fast. Between new tech, rising interest in eco-conscious travel, and travelers craving more unique, immersive experiences, glamping is becoming less of a niche and more of a movement. To stay competitive, we can't just react—we've got to look ahead, even if that crystal ball is a little foggy.

In this chapter, we're diving into the trends that are shaping the next phase of glamping: from smart tools that streamline operations to sustainability efforts that resonate with modern guests to creative strategies for standing out in a saturated market. Whether you're just starting out or ready to scale, staying ahead of the curve is what will keep your sites thriving in this fast-moving, ever-evolving world of outdoor hospitality.

Emerging Technologies: The Future of Smart Glamping

Technology is revolutionizing the travel and hospitality sectors, and glamping is no exception. Innovative solutions are making it easier for hosts to enhance guest experiences, streamline operations, and improve sustainability efforts.

Smart accommodations and automation are at the forefront of this transformation. Smart locks and contactless check-in systems eliminate the need for face-to-face interactions, providing a seamless arrival experience. Voice-controlled assistants like Amazon Alexa or Google Home allow guests to adjust lighting and temperature and even request local recommendations hands-free. Automated climate control through smart thermostats and eco-friendly heating and cooling systems ensures energy efficiency while maintaining guest comfort. Additionally, AI-driven concierge services in the form of chatbots and automated messaging platforms can handle FAQs, suggest local activities, and provide round-the-clock support. I can only imagine what it will be like when AI bots can answer the phone and talk with customers.

Another game changer is augmented reality (AR) and virtual reality (VR) enhancements, which offer interactive and immersive experiences. Virtual property tours enable potential guests to explore accommodations before booking through 360-degree imagery. AR interactive experiences, such as scanning QR codes around the property, can unlock information about local history, stargazing guides, or even nature-based scavenger hunts. Meanwhile, VR adventure planning allows travelers to immerse themselves in simulated glamping experiences before committing to a trip.

In the financial and operational realm, AI-powered pricing and revenue management are helping glamping operators maximize profits. Dynamic pricing algorithms adjust nightly rates based on demand, competitor pricing, and seasonal trends, using platforms like PriceLabs, Beyond Pricing, and Wheelhouse. Predictive analytics powered by machine learning can analyze booking patterns and forecast high-demand periods, allowing hosts to optimize promotions and staffing in advance.

Sustainability is also seeing significant advancements with tech-driven, eco-friendly solutions. Many glamping businesses are adopting solar-powered accommodations, moving toward fully off-grid setups that rely on renewable energy. AI-based energy management systems detect when a unit is unoccupied and automatically adjust power usage to reduce waste. Water conservation technology, such as smart water sensors and rainwater harvesting systems, is helping properties minimize environmental impact while maintaining high efficiency.

As technology continues to evolve, it is becoming an integral part of the glamping experience. From smart automation and AI-driven services to immersive digital experiences and sustainable innovations, businesses that invest in these advancements will lead the market in guest satisfaction and operational efficiency. The future of glamping is not just about nature—it's about blending nature with intelligent, tech-driven solutions that elevate both guest experiences and business performance.

Sustainability Developments: The Push for Eco-Friendly Travel

The demand for sustainable and environmentally friendly travel is growing, and glamping businesses must adapt to meet eco-conscious consumer expectations while reducing their carbon footprint.

- **Recycled and upcycled materials.** Many glamping operators are using reclaimed wood, repurposed shipping containers, and natural building materials for structures.
- **Low-impact foundations.** Floating cabins, tree houses, and yurt platforms that avoid disturbing the natural environment are becoming more popular.
- **Passive design elements.** Building structures that naturally regulate temperature and airflow reduce the need for artificial heating and cooling.
- **Solar panels and battery storage.** More glamping sites are going fully solar-powered, reducing their reliance on fossil fuels.
- **Wind and hydroelectric power.** Locations near water sources or windy environments are incorporating small-scale hydroelectric and wind turbines to generate energy.
- **Biofuel and composting toilets.** Off-grid facilities are incorporating biodegradable waste systems to minimize environmental impact.
- **Zero-waste policies.** Reducing single-use plastics by offering refillable water stations, bamboo toothbrushes, and biodegradable toiletries.
- **Local and organic food sourcing.** Many glamping operators are partnering with local farms and offering farm-to-table dining experiences to reduce food miles.
- **Wildlife conservation efforts.** Glamping sites near protected areas are increasingly incorporating eco-tours, conservation programs, and ethical wildlife encounters.

Sustainability is no longer just a trend—it's an expectation. Glamping businesses that adopt eco-friendly practices will appeal to the growing market of travelers seeking responsible tourism options.

Market Evolution: The Changing Landscape of Glamping

The glamping industry has seen rapid growth in recent years, but what will the future hold? Understanding market trends and evolving traveler preferences can help business owners position themselves for long-term success.

- More travelers are blending work and leisure, seeking glamping accommodations with high-speed internet, work-friendly spaces, and extended-stay options.
- Adding co-working cabins, private office pods, or shared communal workspaces can attract remote workers and long-term guests.
- Listings with "workcation" keywords are seeing higher demand on Airbnb and Vrbo.
- Travelers today value experiences over material things. To meet this demand:
- Offer customized adventure packages (e.g., guided hikes, private stargazing sessions, or survival skill workshops).
- Allow guests to "build their own glamping itinerary" with options like private chefs, personalized spa services, or tailored excursion bundles.
- Use guest data to offer loyalty-based recommendations and exclusive perks for return visitors.

When I first launched Cameron Ranch Glamping, I never imagined how quickly the demand for unique, high-end stays would grow. What started as a dream to create a peaceful escape in nature has now evolved into a business that caters to guests looking for more than just a place to sleep—they're looking for an experience. And lately, one trend has become impossible to ignore: the rise of ultra-luxury glamping.

High-end travelers are more than willing to pay premium rates for exclusivity, comfort, and curated, one-of-a-kind stays. We're talking private infinity pools, gourmet meals prepared by personal chefs, even helicopter transfers for the ultra-remote vibe. Some luxury guests expect the kind of personalized service you'd only find at a five-star hotel—think butlers, concierge-curated itineraries, and top-tier amenities, all nestled in nature. As we look to expand Cameron Ranch Glamping, we're leaning into this trend, making sure each future site raises the bar.

But luxury and family-friendly features aren't enough on their own—guests also crave something truly unique. Themed and concept-based stays have exploded in popularity. From fantasy-style hobbit homes to sci-fi-inspired domes or cabins that feel like you've stepped into a wizard's world, travelers want more than just scenery—they want a story. Some even seek out survival or off-grid training experiences where they can disconnect and learn outdoor skills.

If there's one thing I've learned at Cameron Ranch, it's that standing out requires more than good design. It takes constant innovation, creative thinking, and a deep understanding of what your guests value most. The future of glamping isn't just luxury—it's immersive, personal, and unforgettable.

Adaptation Strategies: Future-Proofing Your Business

With the rapid evolution of the travel industry, glamping businesses must remain agile and adaptable to stay competitive. One key strategy is diversifying booking channels and direct marketing to reduce reliance on third-party platforms like Airbnb and Vrbo. Expanding to niche platforms such as Glamping Hub and Hipcamp, while also investing in direct booking websites, SEO, email marketing, and social media, ensures a steady flow of reservations without excessive commission fees.

Implementing data-driven decision-making is another critical factor in long-term success. Regularly analyzing guest feedback surveys helps refine the guest experience, while monitoring key performance metrics like RevPAR, ADR, and occupancy rates allows for optimized pricing. Utilizing market research tools such as AirDNA and Google Trends can further provide insights into industry trends and competitor performance.

Building sustainable and disaster-resilient business models is essential for future-proofing against environmental challenges. Designing accommodations that can withstand extreme weather—whether hurricanes, wildfires, or floods—ensures long-term durability. Integrating climate-conscious designs and establishing disaster recovery plans adds an extra layer of preparedness. I have already survived hurricanes, tornadoes, deep freezes, and more at my glamping sites, but that doesn't mean we aren't actively preparing for what may come.

Additionally, staying ahead of regulatory changes is crucial in navigating evolving laws related to zoning, short-term rental regulations, and environmental compliance. Keeping track of local policies and considering legal structures, like forming an LLC or obtaining special-use permits, can prevent operational setbacks and allow for seamless expansion.

Last, but certainly not least, fostering a loyal guest community increases long-term profitability and is crucial. Launching a glamping membership program with exclusive perks, offering referral bonuses and seasonal promotions, and creating an engaged online presence through Facebook Groups, YouTube, or behind-the-scenes content all help establish brand loyalty and encourage repeat visits. By staying adaptable and proactive in these areas, glamping businesses can secure their place in an ever-changing market.

Final Thoughts

From what I've seen running Cameron Ranch Glamping, the future of glamping is wide open—and honestly, it's never been more exciting. The opportunities feel endless, if you're willing to stay curious and adapt. Whether it's trying out new tech that makes the guest experience smoother, leaning into sustainable practices, or just paying attention to what today's travelers really want, there's so much room to grow and improve.

What I've learned is that success in this space isn't about having the fanciest tents or the biggest property—it's about being flexible, getting creative, and constantly evolving. The glamping world moves fast, and the hosts who embrace that change—the ones who really listen to guests and aren't afraid to try something new—are the ones who are going to thrive. I'm just getting started, and I already know this industry has so much more to offer.

Lessons from the Field

- **Smart tech is taking over.** AI-powered pricing, smart locks, voice assistants, and VR/AR enhance guest experiences and streamline operations.
- **Sustainability is nonnegotiable.** Off-grid solutions, eco-friendly construction, zero-waste policies, and carbon offset programs attract eco-conscious travelers.
- **Workcations and digital nomads.** High-speed internet, co-working spaces, and extended-stay options cater to remote workers.

- **Luxury and themed stays drive demand.** Ultra-luxury glamping, immersive fantasy/science-fiction themes, and curated experiences are trending.
- **Direct bookings and data-driven decisions.** Reduce reliance on OTAs by optimizing direct marketing and using analytics tools like AirDNA.
- **Future-proofing is essential.** Adapt to climate challenges, evolving regulations, and traveler preferences to stay ahead in the competitive glamping market.

Chapter 18

The Glamping Journey Ahead

This is not a business you want to wing. There's real work involved—planning, budgeting, stressing about weather apps—but if you're up for the challenge, the payoff is worth it. Every decision matters: the type of structure you choose, how comfy the bed is, even the angle of your string lights (yes, people *notice*). The learning curve is steep, but if you lean into it, you'll come out with a business—and biceps—from all the manual labor.

One thing I learned early: Pick structures that actually hold their value. I love a cute canvas tent as much as the next person, but if it starts falling apart after two summers and I can't finance it, we've got problems. Cabins, tiny homes, and park models? Those are your financially savvy besties. Bonus points if they're pretty enough for Instagram but still get approved by the bank.

And I get it—you want to launch five domes and a tree house tomorrow. But slow your roll. Start small. My first build taught me more than any YouTube video or e-book ever could. A test run with one unit gives you space to screw up, fix it, and learn. Plus, it keeps your stress level somewhere below "crying into spreadsheets at 2 a.m."

At its core, glamping is hospitality. And if you're not obsessed with making guests feel special, this might not be your jam. We've had everything from proposals to surprise birthday weekends at Cameron Ranch, and each one reminds me that going the extra mile—like leaving handwritten notes or local snacks—pays off in glowing reviews and return bookings.

Now let's talk marketing. You could have the coolest A-frame this side of Pinterest, but if no one knows it exists, you're just camping alone with your debt. Document the journey. Post the messy middle. Share the funny fails (I once installed a mirror and immediately cracked it—seven years bad luck and a great Reel). Your transparency will build trust, and trust turns into bookings.

As you grow, you'll hit a tipping point where you can't do it all. You'll need help—and not just from your very tired partner, who already painted three accent walls. Building a team and creating systems is what takes you from "fun side project" to actual business.

Scaling is exciting, but doing it without a plan is like trying to pitch a tent during a hurricane.

Also, have an exit strategy. Not to be dramatic, but one day you might want to sell, refinance, or pivot to your next big thing (glamping-themed escape rooms, anyone?). Thinking about your end game from the beginning helps you make smarter decisions along the way.

And seriously—go stay in other glamping spots. Sleep in the dome. Test the composting toilet. See what you love and what makes you say, "Nope, never doing that." Every stay is a research trip with better lighting and a s'more.

The truth? This business is hard. But it's also one of the most rewarding things I've ever done. If you're patient and adaptable and you stay laser-focused on guest experience, you'll build something that not only pays the bills but makes people's favorite memories. And that? That's the real magic of glamping.

Acknowledgments

This guide results from countless hours, unexpected lessons, and the support of a community that made the impossible feel possible. Launching a glamping site and having it succeed right out of the gate was no small feat, especially without the backing of big banks or investors. It took grit, creativity, and a team that believed in the vision from day one.

Thank you to BiggerPockets for giving me the platform to share this journey and to the incredible team that brought this guide to life: Katie Miller, Kaylee Walterbach, and Winsome Lewis. Your trust and collaboration meant the world.

To all the readers: thank you. Whether you're just starting or scaling up, you are the reason this guide was written.

To those who inspired me to take the first step into glamping, and to the team that helps me live this dream every day—Emily Morley, Rose Martorillas, Katy Hartman, Jason Becker, Nichole Ready, Claire Amancio, and every single person who has pitched in at Cameron Ranch Glamping—this is as much yours as it is mine. Thank you to ÖÖD Mirror Houses for taking a leap of faith in partnering with our vision early on.

And finally, to you, the person holding this guide: You can't fail until you quit. The world is a better place with you in it. Go after it.

About the Author

Born and raised in Houston, Texas, Garrett Brown is a seasoned real estate professional with over eight years of experience in the industry. A proud graduate of the University of Houston Hilton College of Hospitality, Garrett has built a successful career as both a real estate agent and investor. To date, he has facilitated over $8 million in real estate transactions and manages a portfolio of income-producing assets valued at over $2 million. Garrett's passion lies in leveraging his real-world experiences to guide others on their journey to financial freedom. Known for his honesty and realistic approach, he avoids empty promises and focuses on the hard work and dedication required for success. Outside of his professional life, Garrett enjoys spending time with his dogs, creating music, experimenting with new recipes in the kitchen, and exploring the best coffee shops in town.

Reference List

Behrisch, Steve. "Maximizing Hotel Profits: The Role of Technology in Pricing Strategy." *The OnRes Blog*. 23 May 2024. https://www.onressoftware.com/impact-of-technology-on-hotel-pricing/.

"Gen Z Travel Statistics, 2025." Condor Ferries. Accessed 25 April 2025. https://www.condorferries.co.uk/gen-z-travel-statistics.

"Glamping Market Size, Share & Trends Analysis Report by Accommodation (Cabins & Pods, Tents, Yurts, Treehouses), By Age Group (18 - 32, 33 - 50, 51 - 65, Above 65 Years), By Booking Mode, By Region, And Segment Forecasts, 2025 – 2030." Grand View Research. Accessed 25 April 2025. https://www.grandviewresearch.com/industry-analysis/glamping-market#.

"Marriott Acquires the Postcard Cabins Brand: A New Chapter for Outdoor Hospitality." *PR Newswire*. 12 December 2024. https://www.prnewswire.com/news-releases/marriott-acquires-the-postcard-cabins-brand-a-new-chapter-for-outdoor-hospitality-302330192.html.

Spitzer, Michelle. "New Disney cabins open at Disney's Fort Wilderness replacing the iconic log ones." *Florida Today*. 2 July 2024. https://www.floridatoday.com/story/news/local/2024/07/01/disneys-fort-wilderness-resort-opens-new-cabins-replacing-log-ones/74267466007/.

BiggerPockets Short-Term Rental Resource Hub page
www.BiggerPockets.com/BookSTRDownloads

BiggerStays YouTube
www.youtube.com/@BiggerStays

BiggerPockets Short-Term Rental Investing page
www.BiggerPockets.com/BookSTRBlog

BiggerPockets Short-Term Rental Newsletter "BiggerStays"
www.BiggerPockets.com/BookSTRNews

BiggerPockets Deal Finder
www.BiggerPockets.com/BookDeals

BiggerPockets Market Finder
www.BiggerPockets.com/BookMarkets

BiggerPockets Agent Finder
www.BiggerPockets.com/BookAgent

BiggerPockets Lender Finder
www.BiggerPockets.com/BookLender

BiggerPockets Property Management Finder
www.BiggerPockets.com/BookPM

SUPERCHARGE YOUR REAL ESTATE INVESTING.

Get **exclusive bonus content** like checklists, contracts, interviews, and more when you buy from the BiggerPockets Bookstore.

Use code **FirstBPBook** for **15%** off your first purchase.

Standard shipping is free and you get bonus content with every order!

www.BiggerPockets.com/STORE

BiggerPockets Newsletter Signup

Want access to more content? Sign up for the BiggerPockets Newsletter using the QR Code below. Covering a range of current topics of conversation, keep in the know about investing in your area.

Sign up now.
www.BiggerPockets.com/newsletter

Short-Term Rental, Long-Term Wealth: Your Guide to Analyzing, Buying, and Managing Vacation Properties
By Avery Carl

From analyzing potential properties to effectively managing your listings, this book is your one-stop resource for making a profit with STRs.

BiggerPockets.com/ReadSTRLTW

Smarter Short-Term Rentals: Build a Dynamic Real Estate Business and Out-Host the Competition
By Avery Carl

In a market of rising interest rates, real estate investors need strategies that maximize returns. That's where short-term rentals shine, delivering 2-3X the cash flow of traditional rentals—but with Airbnb's meteoric growth comes fierce competition. You need a proven framework to stand out and succeed.

BiggerPockets.com/ReadSmarterSTRs

Real Estate Campgrounds: How to Invest in Outdoor Hospitality with Campgrounds, RV Parks, and Glamping
By Heather Blankenship

Discover the wide-open opportunity of outdoor hospitality—a real estate investing niche that delivers outsized cash flow and appreciation with way less competition. Tired of chasing crowded mainstream investments? RV parks, campgrounds, and glamping sites (aka "outdoor hospitality") may be the investing niche you've been looking for

BiggerPockets.com/ReadCampgrounds

The Small and Mighty Real Estate Investor: How to Reach Financial Freedom with Fewer Rental Properties

By Chad Carson

You don't need to build a massive real estate empire to achieve financial freedom, and you don't have to sacrifice what matters to build wealth. Rather than chasing a goalpost that always moves, a small and mighty investor keeps their strategy simple to maximize flexibility and build the life they want.

BiggerPockets.com/ReadSmallandMighty

Real Estate Deal Maker: Winning Strategies to Find & Finance Successful Rental Properties in Any Market

By Henry Washington

The two biggest problems in real estate are finding properties and funding deals—and the solution to both starts here. Are you ready to master the art of finding remarkable properties and securing the funds to seal the deal? Look no further than the expertise of Henry Washington, a real estate investor, influencer, and coach who turned a mere $1,000 into a portfolio of over 100 rental properties in just six years.

BiggerPockets.com/ReadDealMaker

Start with Strategy: Craft Your Personal Real Estate Portfolio for Lasting Financial Freedom
by David Meyer

Simplify your real estate goals with a portfolio plan that fits your personal values, resources, and skills.

BiggerPockets.com/ReadSWS

Real Estate by the Numbers: A Complete Reference Guide to Deal Analysis
by J Scott and Dave Meyer

From cash flow to compound interest, Real Estate by the Numbers makes it easy for anyone to master real estate deal analysis.

BiggerPockets.com/ReadBytheNumbers

Scaling Smart: How to Design a Self-Managing Business
By Rich Fettke and Kathy Fettke

Are you ready to create passive income, free up your time, and grow your business without sacrificing your sanity? In Scaling Smart, RealWealth founders Rich and Kathy Fettke distill more than twenty years of business strategy into an approachable guide to scaling a successful enterprise.

BiggerPockets.com/ReadScalingSmart

Looking for more?
Join the BiggerPockets Community

BiggerPockets brings together education, tools, and a community of more than 3 million+ like-minded members—all in one place. Learn about investment strategies, analyze properties, connect with investor-friendly agents, and more.

Go to **BiggerPockets.com** to learn more!

 Listen to a **BiggerPockets Podcast**

 Watch **BiggerPockets on YouTube**

 Join the **Community Forum**

 Learn more on **the Blog**

 Read more **BiggerPockets Books**

 Learn about our **Real Estate Investing Bootcamps**

 Connect with an **Investor-Friendly Real Estate Agent**

 **Go Pro!** Start, scale, and manage your portfolio with your **Pro Membership**

Follow us on social media!

Join over 3 million investors on BiggerPockets forums. Whether you're a seasoned expert or just starting out, tap into the collective knowledge, confidence, and connections to reach your full potential.

Join the conversation now!

BiggerPockets.com/BookForums

www.ingramcontent.com/pod-product-compliance
Lightning Source LLC
Chambersburg PA
CBHW050904160426
43194CB00011B/2278